ÖSTERMALM

NORRMALM

GAMLA
STAN

DJURGÅRDEN

SÖDERMALM

NACKA

UNCOMMON
STOCKHOLM

UNCOMMON STOCKHOLM

EDITED BY ERIK NORDLANDER

Published by Uncommon Ltd.
in collaboration with
Laurella & Wallin Förlag
www.laurellawallin.se

ISBN 9789197940078
Printed in Italy

The opinions expressed in this book are those of the authors etc.
Facts are deemed correct at time of going to print,
some may be subject to change.

Executive Editor Emma Mattei
Design Jon Banthorpe
Stock Photography:
Tove Freiij *p.55, p.153*
Gustav Elliot *p.111*

Uncommon Ltd.
168 St. Christopher Street
VLT 1476
Valletta, Malta.
www.uncommonguidebooks.com

"Is there anything better than to be longing for something, when you know it is within reach?"

Greta Garbo

INDEX

Tusse at Björkskär by Kai Gullberg

FOREWORD

ERIK NORDLANDER

Founded in the 13th century, Stockholm developed through a mix of awe towards Europe's great nations and the ingenuity of a small and sometimes desolate place. The city's reputation as home to visionaries and forerunners springs from the progressions of the 20th century when the country stayed outside of the two World Wars and took large steps towards democracy and equality.

Stockholm's location on the east coast of Sweden, where Lake Mälaren meets the Baltic Sea, has created a cityscape surrounded by and forked with water. Standing at the waterfront in the centre of town the display of medieval churches, royal and government buildings, adorned palaces and grand houses along the shoreline, makes a fine opportunity for every keen storyteller to begin a tale of Stockholm and its citizens.

For most of us, however, the majestic landmarks and the quaint quarters of Gamla Stan (Old Town) play a peripheral role. Nor are descriptions such as a *Venice of the North* particularly telling, for not only is this an epithet shared between ten other cities in northern Europe, it also has little to do with actual life in the city.

Uncommon: Stockholm is a travelogue created by people who inhabit, or are in other ways connected to, the city; here, we engage in identifying activities, stories, maps and personal routes. It is a guide to our collective historical consciousness, our private spheres and the 12-month city.

Uncommon: Stockholm attempts to bring the reader closer to the rules, quirks and moods of this city; to the densely populated parts of Södermalm, Östermalm, Kungsholmen and Norrmalm; to islands, wastelands and greenbelts; to the imperfections and footprints torn from the perfect plans of patrons and architects.

Supporting the idea of personal journeys and local knowledge, this is a companion for the contemporary explorer; we hope it will prove helpful for your own intimate stories to materialise.

RELATE

MY KARLAVÄGEN

TEXT: **SANDRA BEIJER**

PHOTOGRAPHY: **VIKTOR GÅRDSÄTER**

Just outside the Östra Real secondary school on Karlavägen stands a statue that involved a curious episode with a loveliness of ladybirds. This occurred during the unusually hot summer of 1966. For three days and nights the head, nose, shoulders and torso of the statue, a representation of the author August Blanche, dissolved into a swarm of red and black.

People from the neighbourhood went there to photograph and marvel; naturally, a newspaper wrote an article. My mother tells me this story on a walk one Saturday, when I am 9 years old. For a long time we stand in front of the statue and look at it, quizzically. Both of us are trying to imagine what it could have looked like. I, because I never saw it, my mother, because the memory has faded; perhaps this is why she says it, perhaps this is why she passes the story on to me.

The sandstone statue depicting Blanche is one of many artworks along Karlavägen's own outdoor museum. Sometimes these artworks are vandalised, and the tag usually lasts the summer, until a park keeper tiresomely washes it away, tiresome because he knows that in a month or so new graffiti will appear.

Sibyllegatan junction, a few metres from here, is where I drink the second beer in my life and throw up over *Kvinna med Handspegel* (Woman with Hand Mirror), it's where I text a guy that I dream of getting my first kiss from, and where my friend throws her cell phone up a tree "by accident".

We lean against the bronze statue because the whole world is spinning so fast. We are both 15 and this is the first time I am drunk. According to my friend this is her fourth or fifth time, earlier in the evening she reassured me that she would take care of me if things were to escalate. She did not, of course.

Half the bottle of beer gone, and already I had trouble articulating; my friend ran to the 7-Eleven and bought a pack of Marlboro Lights. Then we headed to Karlavägen, lay down in the September-frosty grass and talked about what we would do with our evening, with our fresh drunkenness. Later we provoked the gang of pretty-boy ninth graders at Gärdesskolan into joining us (I do not remember, but I can imagine their weary glances towards us lying in the grass in short dresses, with grass stains on our stockings) I leaned towards one of the cuter ones and asked for a kiss: "You are drunk Sandra," so he had said.

A half hour later they disappeared and I threw up over *Kvinna med Handspegel*. My friend noticed nothing. Just before midnight I arrived at my front door and vomited again, in the bathroom. My mother stood alarmed at the doorway and repeated what I already knew, as if to enlighten me: "You are drunk Sandra!" she had said.

At the fountain at Karlaplan, which during the summer serves as accommodation for ducks too lazy to head down to the park, a guy in my class lifts me up over his shoulder. Östra Real is where the student cap ceremony is held, and in just a few months we'll graduate from high school and take our first steps into the adult world. It is an unofficial tradition for someone to fill the fountain with washing-up liquid, so that it foams and creates a giant bathtub. There, a guy lifts me up, in my black, skinny Cheap Monday jeans, with my equally black, backcombed pageboy haircut, and he throws me in. The foam sprays over my newly purchased Converse and they applaud. I stand up, screaming "fyyy faaaan!" but all I think is that I've finally become a girl that guys lift up over the shoulder and throw in.

One July evening in the early millennium, my brother calls me. He is standing next to the statue *Man-häst-vagn* (Man-horse carriage) and he says, "there's a baby bird here, you have to take care of it." I walk there with my boyfriend and we are 20 years old and the bird is featherless. It is lying at the corner of Karlavägen and Nybrogatan. We call the Emergency Aid For Birds (there is one, apparently) and they ask us to take it home, wrap it in a blanket and feed it raw mincemeat with tweezers. We call it 'Mark' and it lives for exactly five hours more, until some time around eleven o'clock in the evening, when it tenses its body with a last breath and expires. We wrap it in a pink towel and bury it back where we found it, a silent memorial; we had placed a small cross there, made of two sticks bound together with a few blades of grass that functioned as string. Maybe it's still there, next to the bronze statue of the man and the horse. Hard to know with such small birds.

At Sturegatan junction, in the Handelsbanken office window, stands a marble torso by Christian Berg. It is there that he, who I thought I would grow old and grey with, grabs me and incoherently, sobbing, says he loves me.

"I don't care what you say now I fucking love you." He rests against the window while he covers his chest with his hand, as if running out of breath. We have fought, I have forgotten about what, and the time is around three in the morning and we've been a couple for three months. He is 23 years old and tonight he loves me, and he'll love me for the next four years. I stop in pure amazement and then I gesticulate into the air and yell back, just before my voice breaks: "but you idiot, you know I love you too!"

This is my Karlavägen, my outdoor museum with memories carved into each statue. My avenue, where the green, deciduous trees droop above the gravelled road in July, where one borrows plastic cups from the 7-Eleven, leading a bicycle towards Humlegården, where crocuses bloom in April, where someone takes your hand at Sturegatan junction, where every time you pass Östra Real, and the statue outside, you think of your mother who was once also nine years old, amazed and in awe, wondering how many ladybirds it really takes to make a loveliness to cover August Blanche.

URBAN GARDENER
HOLGER BLOM

A MAN OF HIS TIME

TEXT: **BRITA ÅSBRINK**

Holger Blom was appointed City Gardener in Stockholm in January 1939, that year Germany would attack Poland on the 1st of September. Sweden would remain closed to the outside world until the conclusion of peace in 1945, when the first boat, loaded with bananas, tied up at the dock in Gothenburg.

The Stockholmer and architect Holger Blom was young, interested in art and theatre, and had significant social skills. During his thirty years as City Gardener and head of the park department, he came to develop good contact with the city's politicians, the press and the public, and was inspired by futurism. He was, as one says, the right man in the right place.

After working for an architecture firm in Paris, Holger Blom returned in the summer of 1930, in time for the Stockholm Exhibition. In Paris, he had made the acquaintance of architect and artist Le Corbusier, and this friendship awakened in him an interest in city parks. At the Stockholm Exhibition, social aspects of urban exploration were expressed in the architecture and design of futurism - a recipe for a new future with light and air. The ideologues of the exhibition wanted to introduce good taste and "give good quality to the masses".

Holger started off by putting these influences into his design for the new *Slussen*, between Gamla stan and Södermalm. He was responsible for the Yellow Corridor, the Green Corridor and the Blue Sheds that run underneath the roundabout designed by Tage William-Olsson. The tram was replaced by the modern subway, running south, with *Slussen* as the first stop. Holger designed

the station at Medborgarplatsen and a little later he created *Svampen* (the Mushroom) at the centre of Stureplan, a meeting place for the fashionable crowd in central Stockholm.

When Holger Blom was appointed City Gardener nine years later, he realised the city planners had laid parks where the terrain was difficult or impossible to build on, rather than where they were needed. For Holger, the location and design of the parks held an important place in their function. It was necessary to adjust the park for various age groups and categories, addressing their different needs in a democratic spirit, what was to become known as the welfare state.

The population began to enjoy increased leisure time, and this increased the need for recreation. Large areas of pristine nature were declared suitable for the development of outdoor sanctuaries. These areas had to be easy to approach by bicycle, and in winter on skis. The interest in outdoor recreation and sport enjoyed rapid growth. It became possible for many people to obtain a sports cabin, away from the city centre. Light, air and health became key words. On the radio each morning Kapten Uggla (Captain Owl) held gymnastic exercises: *arms upward stretch - one, two, one, two!*

STOCKHOLM STYLE

Holger Blom took it upon himself to transform parks for contemporary needs, to build new parks in the outer areas, to influence the city planners to include parks in new areas and to activate more life in the parks. He believed parks had to be accessible to all: for children to play; for the elderly's need to rest; for people to play sports and have parties; to give citizens entries to nature, putting well-being and beauty first. This novel approach was quite different in scope to the design and function of former parks, many of which were royal or private, tied to old-style ideals. At the same time, due to the Second World War, importation of plants from Europe became impossible and so Swedish flora and geography were focused upon more intently.

Architects of the park division and artists chose to highlight the landscape typical of the lake Mälaren valley, with its slabs, birch groves and pastures, with distant views and ever-present glistening water. The chief protagonist of this manner, alongside Holger Blom, was the architect Erik Glemme. In Kungsholmen, Erik Glemme transformed the landscape into a two-kilometre route along the waterfront. This relatively narrow strip of 15 metres, with its winding trails, bridges, inlets and a gazebo, was their response to Hyde Park - green grass to tumble around in, sunbathing, playing, listening to music and enjoying picnics. With Holger Blom's executive ability and Erik Glemme's artistic sensibility they were the team that came to give notoriety to Stockholm's parks and squares. This became the starting point for a new park style – *Stockholmsstilen* (Stockholm style), a phrase that would not be coined until 1983.

PARK THEATRE AND ART

A permanent activity in the park life was renewed in the summer of 1942. It was *Parkteatern* (Park theatre) that grew into an institution and in the summertime to delight the citizens, from old to young. For many actors this was also their first experience on stage. *Parkteatern* became itinerant and until today there are shows in the city and suburbs during the summer for free - umbrella, blanket and bring your own picnic!

Perhaps the most important role of the park, according to the father of young children Holger Blom, was to give kids areas to play. He organised *Parkleken* (Park play) for the inner city and in the new suburbs, and he hired female animators in aprons who wrote weekly reports to the park division. Among the letters the park division received from the public, one letter complained that the city kids would be spoiled by bus excursions to the beaches, where they would be treated to milk and buns. This would lead to increased crime and destructiveness of youth, believed the writer acidly.

Also with children in mind, Stockholm's first abstract work of art was inaugurated in Humlegården in 1949. The artwork is named after the Danish artist Egon Möller-Nielsen's daughter Tufsen. Nielsen's abstract sculpture was designed for children to climb up and slide down. This was against the idea of only looking at art. Touching a piece of art was unthinkable! There are a number of *Tufsen* copies in the parks of Stockholm, such as the one in Humlegården, that are still vividly enjoyed by children.

In 1953 Holger Blom became part of the group that was responsible for the transformation of lower Norrmalm, commonly called Klarakvarteren. For the years to come people watched the devastation of demolished houses and deep pits where the subway would be submerged. This was a dream of modernity, with offices and business centres in the city. The demolition of the sculptor Sergel's studio from the 18th century allowed for five high buildings. The residents of perhaps shabby, cheap apartments and small shops were 'relegated' to outlying areas. Relieved, Holger Blom could finally return to his duties as City Gardener.

During his last years as City Gardener, he became embroiled in a people's revolution. Backed by the government, the city planners intended to locate an entry to the underground in Kungsträdgården, a centrally located park with royal ancestry. In order to build the entrance, a group of elm trees were to be uprooted. But the Stockholm residents had had enough of changes and decisions taken without their regard. As the trees were about to be uprooted, a signal went out across the city - come to Kungsan! Youngsters clung to the trees, staying overnight and singing protest songs. Radio and TV followed the events and eventually the police gave up. The elm trees still stand today in Kungsträdgården.

That autumn, when Holger Blom visited a congress in Caracas, Venezuela, a journalist at a press reception approached him and asked "Mr. Blom, tell us about the elm trees!".

PHOTOS: K. G. ROSENBERG REPRODUCED WITH PERMISSION OF TRAFIKKONTORET
STOCKHOLM.

SYSTEMBOLAGET

RULES OF THE DRINKING GAME

TOVE ERIKSEN HILLBLOM, OLLE LANGSETH & KJELL DOKTOROW

Every Friday at around four o'clock in the afternoon, when the brain switches from thoughts of meetings and deadlines to lazy café breakfasts and decadent, wine-drenched dinners in the company of good friends, a familiar and light panicky feeling enters the body. I begin to clock time and make a quick, rough estimate (same as last week and the week before that) of the fastest, least painful way to get hold of that wine for those dinners.

One Systembolaget store is situated close to my office, but they only offer an over-the-counter, queue-ticket system; the other one is slightly further away, but there you can pick out the bottles yourself and this is sometimes a little faster. I know I must get there before they close, and I know that every other person over the age of 20 is, at this moment, having precisely the same panicky feeling, which considerably complicates the task.

So why all this flurry and haste? Well, it is like this - Systembolaget, the only licensed, state-owned stores to sell alcohol in Sweden, close at 6pm or 7pm on weekdays, but on Saturdays they close at 3pm and on Sundays, well, then they don't even open! Unsurprisingly, this has created a nation of hoarders, and during the weekends you might witness the closest thing you will ever get to Soviet bread queues in the western world.

Before closing time on Saturday - the last chance to get a bottle before the weekend - long queues meander outside the Systembolaget stores, and bouncers apply the ancient tavern rule of 'one out, one in'. On a Saturday afternoon in Stockholm, the familiar sound of bottles clinking in the distinctive purple and green carrier bags can be heard all over the city, like festive chimes. Faces flushed by the effort of carrying the weekend's rewards, along with all other shopping, look contentedly down at their bags, as if to say - *We did it. Again.*

Therefore my stress is completely natural. But this innate thirst for alcohol, and the constant fear of being without it, is not only connected to this moment, it is noticed everywhere in our social and night life. How did it happen? To find out one must trail along the winding road of liquor, and trace a story from the old hipflasks to today's colour-coded bags.

It is hard to imagine that just a hundred years ago this was a developing country: a barren and poor, peripheral place, where a quarter of the population had stepped onto ships bound for America in hope of a better life. Those who were left behind devoted their spare time to what people have always done when life felt heavy and the future gloomy: boozing. And it was plentiful in old Sweden. The rich and powerful drank because Russia had conquered Finland (and thus half of Sweden's territory was lost). The middle class drank because the nobility and the upper class did not acknowledge them. The poor drank to make life's edges less sharp, if only for a moment. And so it went.

The state, which ever since the 16th century had had close to omnipotent power in Sweden, realised that if there were ever to be a chance of making this country into something more than a potato field, they would have to address the drinking issue. Almost every farm distilled their own spirits, and anyone who wanted to could start a tavern!

In 1852, the world's first state monopoly store opened in the small town of Falun, which now meant that this was the only place where you could get hold of alcohol. At the same time, the authorities prohibited the distillation of illicit spirits. They then founded state-controlled restaurants, giving themselves the right to kick out drunken guests, and established the rule that alcohol could only be consumed within the four walls of the room.

This strict style proved successful and the system of monopoly stores spread like wildfire across the country. In 1955, all local monopoly stores were merged into what is today known as Systembolaget (commonly referred to as Systemet or Bolaget). The rules for shopping are the same now as they were then: you need to be 20 years of age, sober and there must not be the slightest suspicion that you intend to purchase the drinks on behalf of someone else. The non-generous opening hours are also an important part of the strategy to protect people from their own thirst.

But if the main objective of Systembolaget is to curb the population's drinking at home, the ingenious framework for bars is an attempt to keep the boozing in restaurants at reasonable levels. Perhaps the most remarkable rule is the so-called dance permit. Yes, you read that right. Every venue where people may wish to move their bodies in time to music must apply for a dance permit. The permit also specifies how many people get to dance at the same time. If too many people wish to dance at the same time, it may be that chaos will occur. Violation of the rule, so-called illegal dancing, can lead to the owner being prosecuted and the right to serve alcohol terminated. (Now you might think this is a somewhat outdated rule, but the fact is that as late as 2007 the law was brought up in parliament and the proposition to remove the law was rejected.)

The open-air restaurant space also has strict regulations for the exact area where alcohol may be consumed, which can be traced back to the old rule of the four walls. Often a step to the right or left will determine if you are drinking legally or illegally. If you stand ten centimetres outside the specified area with a beer in your hand and an inspector comes along, the restaurant can immediately lose the right to serve alcohol.

Neither is drinking on an empty stomach recommended - the one that drinks without eating, risks getting drunk too quickly. Therefore, the rule has been introduced that all bars and clubs that serve alcohol must also provide at least three, hot dishes throughout serving time, which is why it is possible to order a nourishing portion of meatballs at 04:55 on a Saturday night.

If you did not know better, with these facts at hand, one could easily draw the conclusion that the nightlife in Stockholm is similar to something you might have experienced in East Germany during the 1970s, but it is quite the opposite: partying is almost sacred, something you plan carefully. This involves well thought-out purchases at the Systembolaget (you need to know exactly what you want) and careful selection of the restaurants, bars and clubs you wish to frequent. When you take partying seriously, you can take it to new heights. And it's even possible to get really drunk.

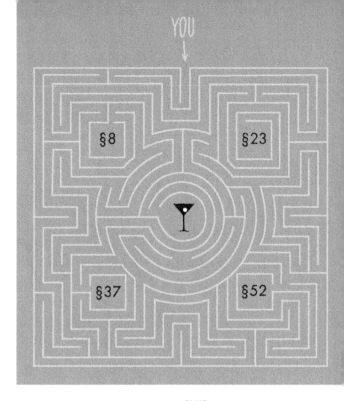

SYSTEMBOLAGET:
PASSAGEN REGERINGSGATAN 44,
STOCKHOLM
A SYSTEMBOLAG WITH STOCKHOLM'S
(MAYBE EVEN SWEDEN'S) BEST VARIETY
AVAILABLE, IN ADDITION TO TRAINED
STAFF, IT ALSO INCLUDES A WINE CELLAR
WITH IMMENSE AND EXCLUSIVE OFFERINGS.
WHY NOT START THE PARTY WITH A BOTTLE
OF CHÂTEAU LATOUR, 2005 AT 11,897
SWEDISH KRONOR?

OUTDOOR SEATING:
BABYLON, BJÖRNS TRÄDGÅRDSGRÄND 4,
STOCKHOLM
VERY COSY AND COLOURFUL WITH
OUTDOOR SEATING, A FRIENDLY
ENVIRONMENT FACING THE PARK, THIS
PLACE MIGHT HAVE YOU BELIEVE THAT
WE ARE FREE TO GO ROLL AROUND WITH
A WINE GLASS IN HAND. HOWEVER, UPON
STEPPING OUTSIDE OF THE ZONE, YOU WILL
BE BRISKLY REPRIMANDED BY THE STAFF.

CLUB:
UNDER BRON, HAMMARBY SLUSSVÄG 2,
STOCKHOLM
UNDER BRON IS LITERALLY UNDER THE
BRIDGE CONNECTING SÖDERMALM AND
JOHANNESHOV, AND DURING THE SUMMER
MONTHS EVERYTHING CAN BE DONE HERE,
FROM DANCING, EATING, PLAYING TENNIS,
ATTENDING A CONCERT, HAVING A BEER OR
HANGING OUT ON ONE OF THE SOFAS. JUST
NOT OUTSIDE OF THE SPECIFIED AREA.

RESTAURANT:
STUREHOF, STUREPLAN 2, STOCKHOLM
WHILE SOME VENUES ONLY OFFER A
DUTIFUL BAR MENU AVAILABLE AFTER
A CERTAIN HOUR, STUREHOF OFFERS
THE POSSIBILITY OF A HIGH QUALITY
RESTAURANT EXPERIENCE, RIGHT UP UNTIL
CLOSING AT 2AM. DRESS FINE AND ORDER A
SEAFOOD PLATTER.

SMORGASBORD WONDERLAND

TEXT: **EDWARD BLOM**
ILLUSTRATIONS: **JOHAN BARRETT**

It is said that the English language has borrowed only three words or expressions from Swedish in the last hundred years: ombudsman, Stockholm syndrome and smorgasbord. Perhaps it is a slight exaggeration but we might say that smorgasbord is Sweden's culinary gift to mankind. It is also the most Swedish of gastronomic practises, a buffet that includes almost every traditional Swedish dish, from herring and gravlax to cold, reindeer steak and meatballs. But *smorgasbord* (sandwich table) has only been referred to as such since the 19th century. Before that it was called *brännvinsbord,*[1] a fact which most Swedes do not know, and under that name this culinary tradition has a much older history.

The brännvinsbord consisted of a small table of appetisers, which for centuries was ingested before all Swedish dinners. During the 16th century it did not include schnapps but consisted of beer, bread, butter and cheese, then as schnapps (brännvin) became a popular drink during the 17th and 18th centuries, it came to play a central role in Swedish gastronomy and eventually gave its name to the whole phenomenon. It was only in aristocratic homes that wine or imported spirits would be served as a complement to the flavoured schnapps.

The table would be laid out long before the guests arrived, functioning rather like today's aperitif, which is served whilst waiting for dinner. As distances were long and communication poor, it could take a long time between the first and the last wagon or sleigh to arrive at the home.

1. *Brännvin is a distilled alcoholic drink often used as schnapps.*
   Brännvinsbord means a table of schnapps.

WOMEN EXCLUDED

The practice of brännvinsbord also came about to fill the need for men to swig back a couple of schnapps before conversing with ladies over dinner, and so women were excluded, though in some parts of the country, women would be present, watching the men as they ate and drank. Then towards the 18th century women began to meet up separately, to drink coffee or liqueurs amongst themselves. When it was time for dinner men and women would unite, and according to custom, the men would accompany the ladies to table.

The brännvinsbord could sometimes also be a way to spend an entire afternoon, playing card games and enjoying conversation, sandwiches and schnapps. Sometimes guests would sit around the brännvinsbord, but it was more common to stand around it, or pick something from the table and sit somewhere in the room, with a plate in one's lap.

Several foreigners who visited Sweden testified about brännvinsbordet, something they perceived as a strange custom. Antonio Possevino, a papal delegate, is responsible for the first written source. He tells about how in 1578 in Sweden, wherever you went for dinner, there would be a small table filled with appetisers, usually butter, bread and cheese. A man by the name of von Bretten, who attended Duke Karl's wedding in Nyköping 1592, depicted how meals were preceded by butter, cheese and bread. Like many others, he paid attention to the tasty, ripened cheeses that were beautifully decorated.

MORE DISHES

During the 18th century, bread, butter and cheese were accompanied by cold cuts, such as slices of smoked sausage or spickeskinka (a salted, cold-smoked ham), and salted herring. At the beginning of the 19th century, the spread began to grow rapidly, with more cold additions such as bacon, tongue, radishes, fish eggs, herring, smoked goose, sardines and anchovies - and it was at this time that the name smorgasbord was adopted, which literally means a table of sandwiches.

An odder variation was reported from Bankeberg, situated in the region of Östergötland, in 1815. There the brännvinsbord consisted of four plates of salad with onion, cucumbers, beets and jam.

By mid 19th century, the smorgasbord began to lose its popularity amongst the higher echelons of society. In 1879, the doctor and cookbook author Charles Emil Hagdahl claimed that it was "no longer considered good manners". Now one would be seated and served by servants, rather than walking around helping oneself from platters, (except in Gothenburg, where the brännvinsbord continued to be practiced by high society who took it to great heights).

Interestingly enough, it is during this time, when brännvinsbord begins to be considered a little vulgar among the upper classes, that it turns into "the broad, wide-ranging smorgasbord" and experiences a huge surge among the rest of the population - now both men and women. And this had much to do with the opening up of the railways.

THE RAILWAYS AND THE GREAT SMORGASBORD

In 1856, the first steam locomotive was put in operation in Sweden, and within ten years Stockholm, Gothenburg, Malmö, Norrköping and Uppsala were linked. Naturally, people traveling long distances had to be offered food and drinks during their journeys, and bistro cars were not introduced until the early 20th century. Passengers would step off when the locomotives stopped to refill with coal and water, but you had to be ready to rush back onto the train again when it whistled for departure. Thus, they could not sit down, await hot food, eat it and then wait for the bill and payment.

The solution for the newly established railway restaurants was smorgasbord, a significantly larger spread than that served as pre-dinner hors d'oeuvres in homes. All kinds of delicacies and drinks were laid out. Guests had to pay a sum in advance and help themselves. When the locomotive howled, they would neck their last schnapps and run towards the train, aspic or piece of cheese in hand. Since railway restaurants were the latest fashion, they set a trend, smorgasbord spread to restaurants all over the country, even to those far from any railway.

SMORGASBORD WONDERLAND

Soon smorgasbord was served in every restaurant of a reasonable standard in the country. Almost every meal began with small delights and schnapps

GRAND HÔTEL'S PORCH
THE MOST EXTENSIVE BUT ALSO THE MOST
EXPENSIVE. WONDERFUL VIEW, SITUATED IN
THE MIDDLE OF THE CITY.
SÖDRA BLASIEHOLMSHAMNEN 8

SOLLIDEN AT SKANSEN
A PERFECT OPTION IF YOU HAVE PLANED
A VISIT ANYWAY IS TO HAVE THEIR
SMORGASBORD FOR LUNCH.
DJURGÅRDSSLÄTTEN 49

OPERAKÄLLAREN
HERE YOU ALSO GET TO TASTE OSKAR II:S
CAKE FOR DESSERT. BEAUTIFUL ROOMS.
KARL XII:S TORG

ULRIKSDALS WÄRDSHUS
RATHER SMALL SMORGASBORD, BUT
VERY GOOD. WEEKENDS ARE A BIT MORE
EXPENSIVE BUT ALSO WITH MANY MORE
WARM DISHES. IDYLLIC AREA FOR BEING SO
CLOSE TO THE CITY.
ULRIKSDALS WÄRDSHUS, ULRIKSDALS
SLOTTSPARK, SOLNA

before the main course. It characterised the Swedish culture to the degree that the Swedish national poet, Verner von Heidenstam, even called Sweden a 'smorgasbord wonderland'.

Schnapps was originally included in the price, and it was not considered polite to take more than three - but there were of course many who discreetly broke this code. A typical smorgasbord would offer unflavoured vodka, some type of aquavit, and wormwood schnapps. Guests helped themselves by turning the small taps on the large canteen, which thanks to the ice-filled compartment in the centre, always kept the drinks wonderfully cold.

By the end of the 19th century the smorgasbord was at its most extensive. The crisp, white linen tablecloths were covered with jars of herring and large dishes filled with salmon, eel and other fish, poached, fried, smoked, dried, in jelly and in liquor. There were many varieties of mayonnaise salads, fish eggs and shellfish, meats from shank to tongue, from pork to venison. On large, porcelain dishes and in bowls of newly polished nickel silver there was poultry, sausages, pâtés, aspics, meatballs, omelettes, casseroles, roulades, cold fried pork, pickled vegetables, salads and ripe, Swedish cheeses.

CRISES AND SUCCESSES

Until 1912 the smorgasbord was always enjoyed as a starter, but during the Olympic Games in Stockholm, foreign visitors ate from the smorgasbord until they were satisfied, and thus refrained from ordering a main course. This was devastating for the restaurant owners who made huge losses and began to withdraw the smorgasbord option. For the Olympic Games management this was embarrassing, and after a couple of days Stockholm restaurateurs imposed a higher price on the smorgasbord-only option. As a consequence, this allowed Swedes who preferred smorgasbord to indulge in their preference without breaking any dining codes.

The summer Olympics in Stockholm contributed further to its reputation, but the smorgasbord's big international breakthrough came at the World Fair in New York in 1939, where the Swedish pavilion proffered a rotating smorgasbord at the pavilion *Three Crowns* restaurant.

In 1914 the heyday of the smorgasbord ended because of war food shortages. Soon after, the Swedish state imposed a total beer ban (everything above 3.5%) and alcohol consumption was restricted to three glasses of alcohol per person, which put the entire restaurant industry in crisis. This was followed by the Great Depression and the Second World War in 1939, causing the government to pass a law banning the serving of smorgasbord, a law that would last until 1949.

When smorgasbord reappeared in the early 1950s, it was of a different kind. The number of the dishes had decreased, but above all, the quality had dropped. Lobster mayonnaise, smoked pig's head, goose breast, venison and salmon roe had been replaced by cheap sausages, prefabricated salads and compressed ham slices.

THE SMORGASBORD RELAUNCHED

The great Swedish chef and restaurateur Tore Wretman called it "gastronomic kitsch" and it was he who would relaunch the classic smorgasbord and restore its popularity. Wretman served a large smorgasbord at the restaurant Operakällaren in Stockholm, intended as a complete meal without main dishes to follow. Now the smorgasbord once again became popular, albeit nowhere near as common as it was before the war.

During the interwar period some restaurants served the so-called *julbord* (Christmas table) during the Christmas holidays. It was a variation of the smorgasbord with some traditional Christmas dishes added (the *julbord* has only grown in popularity in the last 100 years, and nowadays is eaten throughout December).

Today elaborate and diverse smorgasbord are served at only a few places in Stockholm: the Grand Hôtel, Operakällaren, Ulriksdahls Wärdshus and Solliden at Skansen. The *julbord*, however, can be found all over Sweden from 1st December until New Year.

It is my sincere advice to those visiting Stockholm to treat themselves to a real smorgasbord or julbord. It is money well spent to select a more expensive option; it will be an experience you will never forget!

ARKITEKTURSKOLAN

TEXT: **JENNY SÖDERBERG**

When taking a walk in Östermalm you may stumble upon Arkitekturskolan - the school of architecture. It is situated beside Engelbrektskyrkan (one of the tallest churches in mid-town), in between Karlavägen and Östermalmsgatan. If going by metro, the nearest station would be Tekniska högskolan. Arkitekturskolan is raw concrete and brutalist, it is situated amongst brightly-painted, classical buildings, with well-groomed hedges and tidy people. You can't miss Arkitekturskolan!

The building was completed in 1970, a couple of years after the international student uprisings of '68. It was built at a time when parts of inner city Stockholm were being entirely reconstructed, and new ideas behind city planning and architecture were taking hold.

The rebuilding of downtown Stockholm in mid 1900 originated from a competition in the thirties, where amongst 349 other proposals, Le Corbusier was a participant. His idea was to bulldoze great parts of Stockholm, including the entire Gamla Stan, the old Medieval town, and create a futuristic city with high-rises and open spaces, a machine to live in. Le Corbusier did not win the competition, but a modern plan for new Stockholm was devised in the forties.

The new plan was to change the old town of Norrmalm into a modern one, thus changing the movement of traffic and altering the building types. Great parts of Stockholm were demolished during the sixties and seventies, and the inner-city was rebuilt according to these new ideas. The modern planning and buildings were not entirely welcomed by the people.

Architect Gunnar Henriksson was commissioned to design the new school of architecture. The idea behind the new building was to honestly expose how it had been built, to connect and unite, and to give architecture students an

PHOTO BY JENNY SÖDERBERG

PHOTO COURTESY OF KTH

opportunity to participate in the forming of the interior.

Since the building was completed, the school of architecture is ironically voted to be the ugliest building in the city of Stockholm each year. It is said that a majority of the neighbourhood residents want it demolished. And yet it is also a building that is quickly loved by anyone who enters it.

To enter the building you have to climb one of the stairways leading up to the second floor. There are three possible stairways, the main entrance is at Östermalmsgatan 26, and when entering for the first time it's preferable way in.

Once inside, the building will amaze, deconstructing every expectation of how an educational building is supposed to present itself. At the entrance, instead of a main hall or pompous stairway, you enter a triangular room with plain, white floor tiles, and in the middle is a spiral staircase, painted in bright orange. The order here is upside down, every preconception you carry with you will be put into question.

The triangle presents some choices of how to wander through the building. A suggestion is to first take a tour through the student drawing rooms. They are situated in the upper levels. One of the ideas was for the people studying and working here to meet each other spontaneously. To create these meetings, the drawing rooms were made into both a working area and a passageway. This gives the wanderer the opportunity to collide into architecture models, smell the glue and connect with students hovering over laptops and cluttered desks.

The bare interior of raw cast concrete and bricks renders the impression that the building is either not entirely finished, or in the final stages before demolition. In reality it is a forgiving interior, where experiments are made possible by the rough surfaces and unfinished air of the rooms. You can go about painting, sawing, cooking, wallpapering, hanging things from the ceiling, putting up curtains, building a rocket, taking a nap or planting a tree without disturbing any order. It is an interior made for exploration.

It is a rough building, and yet the detailing of it is exquisite: the casting surface of the plants imprinted in the concrete; the bricks placed between the cast pillars; bay windows in wood at the corners of the building; the copper façade meeting the concrete; the formation of the skylights in the lower parts of the

PHOTO BY TOVE FREIIJ

building; everything is considered and precise.

As you move up the building, you will reach the main upper atelier, Övre Ateljén, one of Stockholm's most beautiful rooms; it is full of light and air, with large windows overlooking the church and the tiny square below. Here, impressions from the outside mix with the endless opportunities of a big room. The floor boards are marked by history, with chairs and tables constantly shifting into new formation between classes, with traces of live drawing sessions and plaster mouldings found in the corners. If you spend an entire day here you will experience the movement of light; the best times are dawn and dusk.

The library is at the entrance level, hosting the largest collection of literature and magazines about architecture in Sweden. A good time to visit is when it is snowing or raining outside. Cuddle up in one of the armchairs with a book and enjoy the silence of the room.

A big fire destroyed parts of the school in 2010. Several pavilions surrounding the inner courtyard were burned down. The school building and courtyard are not what they used to be, but this is still the belly of the building. As you enter the triangular room of the entrance hall, you catch a glimpse of it through the glass doors. As the outdoors demand either sun or warm clothes most times of the year, the courtyard is only a promise throughout the winter. But come spring, that promise is fulfilled.

Every visit to the school of architecture should be wrapped up by a moment in the courtyard. Amazingly the cherry tree survived the fire, and in May it blooms. At exam time, the blossoming cherry tree and the sun give the students a reason to flock outside. Preferably buy a coffee at the café and pull up a chair under the pink flowers, take a sip and turn your face to the sun.

The brutalist building is balancing on one limb so drop by soon. The institution is said to be leaving to a newer, more polished building. With this departure the building's purpose will soon be lost, its future is uncertain. This gives the inside a special aura, it occupies a hole in time, where everything is still and yet moving.

ECHOES FROM HÄGERSTEN

TEXT AND PHOTOGRAPHY: **SUSANNA ÖSTERBERG**

VINTERVIKEN: A BLAST FROM THE PAST

Vinterviken, a few kilometres south-west of town, holds a story of 19th century innovation that had a significant impact on the modern world which surprisingly few people, not even Swedes, know of.

Passers-by may be curious about the tunnels and bunkers in the cliffs surrounding the bay, until they learn that these were once used as testing grounds for explosives. At the far end of the bay, a tall, old chimney rises above the trees, a reminder of the industry and ground breaking discoveries that took place here more than a hundred years ago.

The large red-brick building that now houses a café and conference hall was once a factory where sulphuric acid was made for the production of dynamite. It was here that Alfred Nobel (1833-1896), the inventor of dynamite and perhaps the most famous Swede throughout history, set up his industry in 1865. In contrast to prior explosives, dynamite was a lot safer and easier to handle. It played a central role in revolutionising construction and mining, and thus helped advance modernisation.

This narrow valley, surrounded by forest and high rocks, was a perfect location for Nobel to carry out his dangerous work. The factories operated here from 1865 to 1920, after which business was moved elsewhere. It was Alfred Nobel's wish to use the wealth he had accumulated over his lifetime to set up a fund for recognising those who make important contributions to science, literature and the promotion of peace, and he created the Nobel Prize, regarded as the most prestigious of all awards.

After the use of the land in Vinterviken ended in the 1980s, the buildings that were once Nobel's factories were neglected and left to decay. It is only recently that the one remaining factory was restored. Nowadays, Vinterviken is a quiet place with nearby housing estates. Besides the café, the other buildings are today used as studios by painters, sculptors and furniture designers. Many Stockholm inhabitants come here for a pleasant stroll around the bay, a swim in lake Mälaren, or perhaps a walk into town on the ice in wintertime.

TELEFONPLAN:
WORKING CLASS QUARTERS TURNED FASHIONABLE SUBURB

Telefonplan is, as the name suggests, dominated by the functional, industrial architecture of the major telephone and communications company LM Ericsson. The main streets have names relating to the company's operations (microphones, telephones) or prominent characters in its history (LM Ericsson, HT Cedergren). Many of the buildings are classified as historically significant, meaning owners are legally bound to preserve the exterior as they were originally built. In the late 1930s, Ericsson established itself here. The company's buildings stood out with their ultra modern style, an architecture that was part of the company's ambition to secure the wellbeing of the employees. Workers' families were given apartments in the surrounding area. Likewise, these flats were built according to the functionalistic spirit, with windows facing two opposite directions, allowing lots of light to flow through. They were also equipped with a separate kitchen and bathroom, a rarity for the working-class population at the time. Little by little, the area became something of a mini Ericsson town, with the employees living and working here, spending their leisure time in the cultural centre, Midsommargården, which is still active today and was commissioned by LM Ericsson to be built in the square close to the metro station.

Alongside the manufacturing and production of telephones, innovative experiments in design and technology were carried out inside the facilities. One product in particular was so successful that it has been ranked by MoMA as one of the finest achievements in 20th century industrial design: the famous Ericofon, better known as the 'cobra telephone'. Designed in the late 1940s, it incorporated the dial in the handset, and is seen as a forerunner of the modern mobile phone.

With the rise of information technology, manual labour gave way to office work, and large parts of the facilities were not needed anymore. As a result, Ericsson gradually began moving out in the 1990s. By 2003, one of Sweden's most reputed art schools, Konstfack, had already moved into the old premises, and many other creative design companies soon followed their example. And so the transformation of Telefonplan was complete, when Ericsson left the area altogether in 2009. The old workers' houses are now inhabited by young families and students.

The tall, red brick building next to the route E4 (stretching from the north of Finland to the southern tip of Sweden) is a landmark in Stockholm's cityscape. Once the headquarters for Ericsson's offices, it was designed by Anders Berg in the 1960s, who is also the architect behind Globen (the globe); the office spaces are being changed into 365 new living estates for young people, which is a welcome initiative considering the shortage of flats in Stockholm.

A striking fusion of past and present is the 72-metre tall, slim grey tower that first greets your eyes when you exit the metro station. The telephone tower, which was originally used for short wave radio experiments and research, has been turned into an art project called *Colour by Numbers*. The windows along the body of the tower are an interactive and permanent light installation that brightens up the dark skyline every night. Want to try it yourself? Just make a free telephone call to 020-720 200 and follow the instructions to change the colour of the tower yourself!

GÖRING GOES INSANE IN ASPUDDEN

Hermann Wilhelm Göring (1893-1946) was the most powerful man in the Nazi regime after Adolf Hitler. He was also a notorious junkie and had an on and off battle with drug abuse his whole life. It was his Swedish wife, Carin, who got him help and checked him into a nursing home in Aspudden.

After the capitulation of Germany in 1918, Göring left the country in hope of better career opportunities. With his experience as a fighter pilot and reputation as a war hero, Göring eventually got a job at the Swedish airline, Lufttrafik AB, in 1919. Not long after, he met his Swedish wife to be, Carin Kantzow, and they

fell madly in love. She was already married and had a child but was so struck by Göring, that she got divorced and moved to Munich with him.

Göring's addiction to morphine developed as a result for treating the pains from injuries suffered in the failed coup d'etat in 1923, known as the Beer Hall Putsch, the first attempt by Hitler and his Nazi Party to seize power. Again, Göring left the country, however this time he was forced to flee and was not granted amnesty until four years later. During his exile, Göring and Carin eventually took refuge in Sweden. By this time, his drug addiction had worsened and his wife insisted on him being committed to a treatment facility. Göring agreed, and was checked into Aspudden's nursing home on the 6th August, 1925.

The following letter and journal cast light on Göring's unstable disposition. These documents demonstrate his sinister character, and also correspond with the psychological profile that was carried out twenty years later during the Nürnberg trials.

One of the nurses tending to Göring wrote a letter to her chief, in which she expresses revealing details about his behaviour and condition during his stay at the hospital. On 2nd September, 1925 she writes:

Hereby I want to provide some information on Captain von [sic!] Göring's behaviour during his last two days of his stay in Aspudden's nursing home. Early on, time proceeded calmly, although he was extremely irritable and insisted on his medicine ration. On Sunday the 30th of August, Captain Göring's demand for a greater dose of Eukodal became very forceful. He absolutely insisted on getting the quantity, as decided by him. At around five o'clock in the afternoon, he broke into the medicine cabinet and self-injected two syringes of 2% Eudodal solution. Six nurses could not control him, and he became threatening. Captain Göring's wife, who was present, requested most firmly that he get what he wanted. She feared that in his rage, the Captain might even kill someone. Following permission by chief physician Eneström, he was given 0,10 Luminal x 4 and 0,75 [measurement illegible] x 2 of morphine.

Monday 31st August, Dr. Eneström yourself were present, and Captain Göring said he was willing to follow the prescription. At around ten o'clock on Tuesday, the patient became very quarrelsome and again demanded medicine. He rushed up, got dressed and wanted to get out so that he in one way or another could end his life, as he, who had killed 45 people, now did not have any other choice but to take his own life. As the front door was locked, he could not get out, but went up to his room and armed himself with a cane, which turned out to contain a sort of rapier. When a man arrived to help, Captain Göring became further enraged and readied himself to attack unless the man did not leave immediately.

After repeated injections, the patient remained in bed, constantly requesting more. When the police and firemen arrived at six o'clock, he refused to comply. After extensive negotiation, the patient had to be handled by force. He did indeed try to resist, but soon found it to be useless.

Yours respectfully,
Anna Törnquist

Due to Göring's violent and erratic behaviour, he was moved to an asylum for the insane in Långbro, not far from Aspudden. A journal excerpt from his stay there records Göring's mental state:

Långbro Asylum 2/9 – 7/10, 1925:
difficult, discouraged, moans, cries, anxiety, tiresome, irritable, uneasy, loquacious, possibly subjected to 'conspiracy of the Jews', hateful towards Dr. Eneström for the internment, E. bribed by the Jews, suicidal thoughts, himself 'a politically dead man if the internment is known about in Germany', i.e. through his former nurse; exaggerates withdrawal symptoms, hysterical disposition, egocentric, Jew-hater, devoted his life to fight against the Jews, has been Hitler's closest man, (...), intimidating, smuggled in an iron weight as weapon; visions, voices, self-loathing.
(free translations)

In the 1940s a school was built next to Aspudden's nursing home. Soon thereafter, the building was taken over and used as classrooms instead. It was known by the locals as 'the green house' and 'the Göring house' and was demolished in 1969.

FOLKLORE CENTRUM

TEXT: ISRAEL YOUNG
PHOTOGRAPHY: EMELIE LINDGREN

I was born in New York City, 1928, in the Lower East Side, on 110 Ludlow Street. The neighbourhood was mostly Jewish working class families. Lots of markets, more Jewish theatres than in all of NYC, lots of kids to play with, occasional visits to local synagogues. Mama singing Jewish songs and doing all the house work. Papa working in bakeries and bringing home warm bread at 5 or 6 am. Mama would have a warm meal waiting for him and my brother (Oscar), and I would taste the delicious soup and meat that she cooked for Papa. We never called them by their Christian names: Pola and Raphael from Poland. Only Mama and Papa.

A few years later we moved North to the Bronx as we got six months free rent to help fill all the new tenement buildings coming up. Our street was so poor that President Roosevelt and his cortege drove down our street to ensure votes for his second, third and fourth successful terms as the President of the USA. We obeyed our teachers automatically. We knew the local cops by their names. I was smart, yes, but the girls had higher IQs, and at the graduation, right after the USA joined World War Two, I received the first tragedy of my growing intellectual life. Eleven of us on the stage to get awards. One gal got the French award, another the Science award, and yet others, History, Literature etc. I was the last one on the stage, without a clue as to my award. Yep! I got it for Physical Excellence. Fan! Thirty-five years later I meet a Boston Professor of Mathematics, in Sweden. "Glad to meet you again, Izzy. I loved to see you climb the ropes like an ape in the school gym!" I was glad at finding out how lucky I was to be noticeably healthy.

I am admitted to the best High School in NYC and someone researching me found that I got the lowest grade anyone ever got and graduated. I got into Brooklyn College after taking a second test and I did well as I do when up against the wall. I never graduated. The remembrances I have are the Green House, teaching square dances at lunch time in the Lounge and staging a quadrille for a performance of John Gay's *The Beggar's Opera!* I was proud that the opening night, in London, was almost exactly 200 years earlier than my birth. Soon it will be 300 years, so that's how I learned that a century is not a long time. I listened to the Hit Parade on the radio, and kept a journal on the winners for several years. Soon after I got stuck on Square Dance, I started to meet all the singers and dancers. I started to buy books, reading all I could find on the subject. But I still had no job whatsoever so I was a summer waiter for 14 summers in Upstate New York. But I could teach folkdances once a week and so on.

I used to hang around Book Row, East of Greenwich Village. While adding to my library, I would help out in the book shops; the first love of my own. I still had no job so I put out a catalogue of books on Folklore and it was a success (how could I have known that?). I helped out at several bookshops. I issued a second catalogue. Still a waiter during the summer and part of the winter. Suddenly a book shop on Macdougal Street became available.

My own life began, even if it was idiotic to try to sell serious books, records and magazines on an already commercial street far from the culture I was dreaming, I met musicians, artists, poets and now I was one of the shop owners greeting friends, visitors and customers. A well-known promoter calls me from Chicago and asks if I could put on a concert with Pete Seeger's sister, Peggy, then living in England, the coming Friday. I agreed and I put on my first concert like a professional. Six or seven hundred concerts followed until Pete Seeger visited Sweden and enjoyed two Swedish fiddlers (Ole Hjorth and Björn Ståbi), so much so, that he invited them to the 1968 Newport Folk Festival, where the listeners accepted such music from other lands. I loved their music, too, and said, come to NYC and I'll have you on my radio program, and arrange a concert, and you can stay in my apartment. I also arranged a recording on the Elektra Label for them. They invited me to Sweden and I enjoyed many aspects of Sweden that I took part of.

I was together with Catherine, a French Exchange Student. We spent time in NYC, France and Sweden, but we moved to Sweden 1973. Our daughter,

Philomène, was born a year later. As I say: there was no baby in NYC - nor in Paris. But there sure was a baby in Stockholm - Philomène.

Less than a year later I opened the Folklore Centrum near Sveavägen and people were so glad to see books and recordings and, as well, concerts of Swedish folk music, and, of course, me, and it was not only because of my reputation, I already had a reputation when visiting other music shops in Sweden. Owners would say: "Please, Mr. Young, don't ask why we don't sell Swedish folk music - ask my accountant instead!" I had no credit to speak of but I was treated happily by companies selling books and records - in fact, 100% credit - something I never had in the USA. I was soon putting on concerts at Teater 9 down the block. Two or three years later I had to leave my store-front as I could not pay the monthly rent of 732 kronor. I was given space at Teater 9 in their ticket office - damned odd but the neighbourhood accepted it gladly. Teater 9 closed down as the block was to be made into apartments and fancy stores, everything I had was sitting in a bus that the theatre let me use. So my life's work was parked on the street. A wonderful fan of mine got me a store-front on Götgatan: no contract, no rent, but I was soon moved to another location, and then to 3 or 4 other shops. I worked for years on a now big business street. A good friend steered me to an available storefront on Wollmar Yxkullsgatan, which is now the longest I've ever been in one place, nearly 30 years. I have many friends but I hardly ever meet professional musicians, but they sure want to play in my place as I forbid any sound system, which means I am doing it for my own personal pleasure and many well-known musicians played for me (30-40 seats) because they could hear themselves, something impossible in a 'thousand' Stockholm bars. More 'tourists' than ever look inside the store, film me and ask me to pose with their company. I am a proper shop-owner. I ask about their interests. "Everything." Liars. I refuse to entertain with my 179 stories about Dylan. Go to a Dylan concert and learn for your self, I say. They leave, thank God, and I can breath again.

A fifteen-year-old girl walks in and asks for Izzy: "I'm Izzy." She is surprised, as I do not look like a great promoter, manager or agent. She has already written her first song and asks me to send it to Dylan for her, dreaming that sending it with my street address would make some of her dreams possible. I do offer her

Dylan's box number but she wants his *private* address. I say that I write to Dylan at Box 2343454939. She quickly leaves with a broken heart. People send me their recordings and expect a quick positive response. A guy walks in to tell me that a lady friend of his would love to play in my emporium. I ask if she can walk. People call from everywhere for contacts when they are about to leave Sweden on vacation. At least 100 such cases a year, and none of them would dream of coming to even one of my concerts, sort of bribing me, so that I would be forced to help them.

I have many sources of information on what is happening just about everywhere. To them I am just a paid Information Officer. I usually invite them into my storefront to go through all the local folk magazines I have, and books with hundreds of names of clubs and others that work with folk music. They all assume that I am a member of a State Culture Agency and so no need to thank me for anything I might show them. A lady comes in and asks what I "do" (at the Folklore Centrum). I tell her a few things. But it is more she wants and I have no idea what she needs to be made happy. She turns around and says "Lycka till", (I wish you luck!) which is worse than saying "fuck you!". I am glad as she will never visit me again. Someone comes in and wants to do a concert, with keyboard, electric guitar, and other tools one presses or steps on to change the tones and increase the available noise. I say "sorry" so that means he has to find another way to start his career. I also tell him to be ready to guarantee 40-45 seats to the club owner for the privilege of letting him sing for a public.

I was in London last year and read poetry at a new club. I got more reaction than I get in a year in my loved Stockholm. A lady comes in with a sheaf of poems and wants me to correct her English translation, on the spot. Her stuff is more important than my life. A large park calls me and wants me to do a public Square Dance (one of my things) and tells me, happily, that I will get a chance to show what I do to a large public.

And lastly, I do what I do for the fun of it. I am still a fun-loving Jewish boy who grew up in the Bronx, NY - never changed or tried to change - did all he did for his loving attachment to live music - and hundreds of friends all over - always surprise visits that keep him alive - and his open parties every five years. Now that he is 85 he has decided to have open house parties every tenth year.

REVIEW

NOVEMBER

TEXT: **JACOB BOHLIN**
PHOTOGRAPHY: **TOVE FREIIJ**

When I wake up, it will probably be bright. If I'm lucky, a little sunlight will slip through the window, hit the bookshelf and light up the room, even if only briefly. In late November the sun doesn't rise until most people have already had their oatmeal, coffee and are already well on their way across town. There is a two-hour window of proper daylight, between 11 and 1, when the sun reaches over the rooftops, all the way down to the streets. When it does, the Art Deco façades across my street, Robert Almströmsgatan, are each coloured a different pastel – from burnt sienna to pistachio. Right now, all is steeped in indigo, indistinguishable. For the next two months, each day will be even shorter than today.

When I wake up, it is still dark. A train rattles by, generating blue flashes of light as the current collectors glide along the icy cable. I make tea, as I always do, whether I drink it or not. Dog owners walk by outside, their dogs melting the frost on the low iron-fences with their steaming urine. If I go outside today, it will be to Stadsbiblioteket, the City Library on Sveavägen. In my eyes, it's the most beautiful building in the city. And it's bright in there. Some days I go straight to the history department. There are books on the history of eunuchs, torture, architecture and civilization in general. I sit down at a desk, complete with a small, green-shaded reading light, just as it should be, and I browse. If I don't go outside today, I'll play my clarinet, and look out the window.

Falling back asleep after breakfast is a great thing to do. I dream of jet-skis, and black water full of slithering vegetation. A cathedral in the archipelago is Gothic and grey, and flooded with black water. Stuff slithers between my toes; the water is not cold at all. When I wake up the second time, a little sunlight is slipping in, hitting the bookshelf.

If I go outside, it will be somewhere bright. Somewhere where I can get some air beneath my feet. It would be nice to get high. High up, in a tall building with windows as wide as its walls. I used to see a girl who lived in Skrapan on Södermalm, on the ninth floor. That's well over the rooftops of the surrounding buildings. Her room was bright and small and white. Everything was white. The stainless steel lift took forever to the top floor, where we walked hallways to windows facing each cardinal direction. To the south, the Globe Arena was swelling like a giant button mushroom. To the north, the high-rises at Hötorget were lit up, slowly shifting colours along with the mood of Stockholmers. The old and new Årsta bridges to the west – one resembling an antique aqueduct, the other a giant, grey striped serpent – lay parallel, trafficked and, at this distance, perfectly silent. To the east, the church Sofiakyrkan cut through the reddening canopy on its hilltop like a diamond still partly in the rough. To go outside today, I'll have to dress warm.

If I go outside, not towards the library but in the opposite direction, I'll cross the bridge. On the bridge, air is beneath my feet. Air and trains. The air is also in my face. It gains good speed over the rail yard and the water. When the sky is pretty, people stop here to gaze. Right on the bridge, they stop their bicycles in their tracks to take pictures with their phones. In summer, the subarctic sunsets paint the clouds cherry-apricot for over an hour. Peach and strawberry too. Should I cross the bridge today, I'll have to keep a finger on the side of my hat, to keep it from blowing away.

Across the bridge is Kungsholmen, one of the bigger islands on which Stockholm is built. The beer is cheaper there, the traffic more dense. It's louder, and it smells different. I'd hardly ever go there if it weren't for the supermarkets. They're better on Kungsholmen. Bigger. Less expensive. Even late in the evening I've seen Daglivs bustling with customers: Whole families shopping at night; fathers on leave from their parental leave, wives bruising the avocados, small children damaging tomatoes. And that piss-stained old poet again, mumbling through his greying beard, asking grocery boys for discounts and their phone numbers. If I go shopping today, it will be at Prisextra. Both places are about equally bright.

O, greatest Sun, how loved you are! Whenever your rays shine and raise a mist so high and fine; when you warm our cheeks through winds of biting cold; winter days when your complexion is that of an angel! When you boldly stroll in late, great diva that you are, ceaselessly circled by suitors; when you leave early, as if rushing forth to less worldly duties! Whenever you keep us longing; whenever you leave us hoping; whenever you bless us, Mistress, with your presence!

Our love for you is unconditional; towards us: your eternal indifference. Loyal dogs of yours are we: any crumb from Mistress' hand, devoured in gratitude and glee. O, all-warming light of days! Life-giver and to-death-burner! Great desiccator of deserts desolate and dry! Mighty melter of glaciers! Mammoth motor of all menacing storms! Please, say you love us back and smile! And please, just once: Can't you stay a little longer while?

I need to find a place both bright and warm, preferably without a heap of other drawbacks. The brightest bar in Stockholm must be Gondolen, near Slussen. Deriving its name from an airship's cabin, the gondola, it hangs in mid-air some 30 metres above the roundabouts and quays below. That's certainly a bit of air beneath my feet. Also, its windows are about as wide as its walls. Perhaps I should try going there for a couple of hours around noon someday soon. I'm afraid though, that at those hours the place might be full of lunching careerists, tourists, dentists and what have you, chasing off any tranquillity. However, I do remember the barman knowing how to serve cocktails of decent quality. I also remember them knowing to charge for said cocktails without unnecessary modesty.

The second place that comes to mind is Hotel Nobis on Norrmalmstorg. Their lounge - a glassed-in 1880s courtyard, mostly painted white - is bright even at night: full, but not unfashionably so, of champagne-sipping conversationalists, actually lit up to a degree approaching daylight. In the daytime it can be a very tranquil place, not patronised by anyone but the odd laptop-tapping business visitor. One afternoon I went there to read, and found it completely comfortable. When I had chosen an armchair and made myself at ease - neither sooner nor later - a girl showed up in the room, asking if she could offer me anything from the bar. The coffee came served in a small pot of stainless steel; cup, saucer, milk and sugar neatly on the side. It tasted fine, in itself nothing out of the ordinary,

but at 45 kronor, was probably one of the most highly priced filter-coffees in the so-called free world. However, the impeccable service and rare music-free ambience made the price fully tolerable, if not exactly encouraging to make such visits a habit. When I think about it, that just might be the point. The address 'Norrmalmstorg', by the way, is featured in the Swedish version of the board game Monopoly, as the most highly valued property. And anyone familiar with the classic game is aware of the consequences of visiting a hotel built on that square of the board. Nevertheless I should pay them another visit; taking into consideration both the night and day light-conditions, the lounge at Hotel Nobis may very well grab a leading position among Stockholm's brightest establishments.

It's the fifth of December. When I wake up, the city outside my window has changed. Compared to a month ago, the glances of pedestrian eyes are directed noticeably lower. Most striking are the changes in shape and colour, but even through closed windows a slight change is audible in the familiar sounds and noises of the neighbourhood: a muffling effect, much more pronounced than I had remembered it, lie over the rattling of each passing train, over barks of dogs and the occasional bangs of closing rubbish bins. To the eye, contours have become softened: every shape covered in thick duvets, smooth, seamless and white – familiar, but barely. Outside, every visible horizontal surface is perfectly white, any tyre tracks already covered anew by the still falling snow. Many neighbours seem to let their cars rest today, over-snowed in their parking spaces. The heap of rubbish in the gutter outside my window – a blend of empty cigarette packs, tabloids showing their true nature as they dissolve into pulp, and a few plastic bags of the type commonly used by dog owners – which over the last month or so has accumulated on top of a burst dumpster bag full of construction debris is, though still not cleaned up, at least out of sight and so out of mind. From the south, the Sun finds a passage through the otherwise overcast sky, sending its beams sideways under the clouds, lighting up the gentle snow-fall in pale white-gold. On a day like this I just have to go outside for a while, preferably before the Sun begins to set again, just behind the rooftops.

ARCHIPELAGO IN TRANSFORMATION

TEXT: **TOMAS TJAJKOVSKI**
PHOTOGRAPHY: **ÅKE E:SON LINDMAN & GÖRAN UHLIN**

Real Swedes shoot their elk, fix their own cars and build their own houses. With agrarian society only a generation away, many Swedes still have a natural propensity to practical work and find pleasure in carpentry, cooking and tinkering. Lutheran ethics and high taxes on labour have also contributed to this; many prefer to do the work themselves, rather than pay for help from others. In the finer residential areas outside Stockholm, you often see owners of fancy cars on their knees with a floor cloth and a bucket; seems they'd rather do it themselves than pay 200 kronor at the car wash.

Even Swedish summer holiday houses have something Lutheran about them. Established doctors spend their free time building new porches, company directors carry latrine buckets to the compost. In this way the holiday house has also served as a spiritual return to peasant roots, where one would live simply with nature and do good. Out in the woods to pick berries. Out on the lake to net fish. Down on the ground to cultivate.

In my daily work I meet people who have bought or are going to buy summer houses in the archipelago. We now see that something is changing. The old type of outdoor enthusiasts, fishermen, DIY guys and dry privy-emptiers, are about to be replaced with something as odd as the bon vivant. They choose their plot if it is a sunny spot, rather than because of good fishing waters nearby, and listen to *Spotify* in surround sound systems, rather than to bird twitter.

The new settlers prepare gourmet meals in steam ovens and digest on lounge furniture under shady trellises. They pour champagne from the wine cooler and relieve themselves in lavish water closets made out of the natural stone. Some do not even own boats, and instead see the jetty as a nice place to install a jacuzzi.

What unites all these temporary islanders is a longing for the summer idyll; a long autumn, winter and spring of waiting, with memories of childhood's endless holidays. This is time to spend with the children, decorating and cultivating plants, going on excursions and picnics. This is when we swim, fish and read books received last Christmas, when we drink and eat excessively and still find time to jog. Siblings and their offspring visit, in-laws linger and the neighbours never go home. When the best friend from the past comes by with his family. And when half the day is spent shopping, cooking, washing up, cleaning up, packing up, making the beds...

The Stockholmare's summer house is the epitome of the good life; a fulfilment of stored up dreams. A magical place where everything is to be lived out during a month, then closed up again, to be empty for the other eleven. Beautiful is short here in Sweden. The modern Stockholmare's dream of the holiday house is all about personal comfort and relaxation. However, the old Swedish mill society, and later that of the social democracy, norms remain prevalent in the aesthetics. Here it is important that you fit in. To stand out, or plume oneself, is taboo.

The resident island population's cottages painted with Falu red paint and white corners were charming but similar to each other and cottages found throughout Sweden. In the 60s, when the holidays were made longer and ordinary folk could afford to buy summer houses, thousands of new homes in the archipelago were built. These so-called sportstugor were created in a common format – simple, practical boxes without extravagances, that came delivered in kits.

Now that the new generation create their dream homes it has become the subject of suspicious glances and neighbourhood feuds can rage against the new rich, perceived by some as destroying the archipelago with their vulgar houses. But the new houses in the Stockholm archipelago are contemporary interpretations of the old aesthetic norms. Good taste is supposed to be consistent with discretion and if you can afford extravagance, you should not show it to others.

Out in the country, most holiday homes are still built like the chalets of the sixties, or copies of old cottages with porches, mullioned windows and gingerbread work, but round the larger cities, the slightly diffused concept

'nyfunkis' (new functionalism), has been established. It is a term that in reality means clumsy houses with offset blocks, emphasized lean-to roof and large glass surfaces, in more or less imaginative arrangements. Although the houses are free of decoration, they are distinctly different to the light elegance of their modernist precursors.

The people seeking a designed archipelago-house are looking to create a dwelling that they can maintain throughout their lives, a house that their children and grandchildren can inherit. What is important for them is a timeless form that does not dominate over nature, using materials that are pleasant on the eye and can survive the wear of time, without either retro romance or spectacular design for its own sake, and a good, traditional build-quality with a solid wood frame, good insulation and quality wooden windows.

The architect-designed houses that now emerge in the archipelago blend in and subordinate to nature. The best ones have simple and sleek lines, are built in local natural materials, have wooden facades in shades of grey, and plenty of glass to reflect the outside. Ornaments, decorations and round details are as taboo today as ever. The architect's challenges are very much about creating a beautiful house that suits both a sensitive archipelago of rocks and outcrops, clients that do not want to stand out too much, hard shore protection rules, zealous building permits administrators and concerned neighbours. The interior tends to be white and unadorned, with durable, solid floors in local woods such as pine or oak, white-stained or white-soaped floors. On the walls pine panelling, painted white, gives a relaxed rural feeling. Social spaces are built around cooking, and large, sliding sections of glass blur the boundary between indoors and out.

Swedish architects who are making their mark include Thomas Sandell for his renaissance of the traditional cottage with pitched roof, Anders Landström for his way of working with solid wood, both exterior and interior, Waldemarsson & Berglund for their ability to adopt and shape their buildings to the surrounding nature, Tham & Videgård in their search for new expressions of traditional materials and Kjellander & Sjöberg for their reinterpretations of American modernism.

FLIGHT PATHS

TEXT: **MATS GOTHNIER**
ILLUSTRATION: **MATTIAS BÄCKLIN**

APPROACH TO STOCKHOLM

Flying in over Stockholm at night one might wonder where the city begins and where the city ends. Can you even land in this thick darkness? Large desolate, forests and lakes reach far into the city centre and the illuminated habitation appears to be randomly thrown out into the landscape. Had not our main airport Arlanda lain beside the winding, brightly lit European Route 4, one could almost believe that something was amiss when landing.

It is different for the birds. For them, Stockholm must feel like a generous city, packed with fine landings; the city and suburbs are laid out like a star, where habitation has developed along traffic corridors and in between are inviting, lush forests and sparkling, lake systems.

LIKE A PRINCESS CAKE AMONG CRUSTS

Nature around Stockholm consists largely of lean, flat rock areas with conifers. The city's parks instead offer lush, deciduous greenery. This, combined with the parks often located on ridges (which historically have been difficult to build on) makes them, seen from a distance, rise as alluring light green islands on the city skyline. For birds that approach from the south in spring, a city park might therefore seem like an alluring *Princess Cake*, a popular cake here in Sweden that is covered in green marzipan, among crusts.

On some days the parks are teeming of birds that must feed before they move on. There are many advantages for the birds in the city. In winter, it is a few degrees warmer and the lighting makes it possible to find food round the clock.

Some have also expressed the belief that there are fewer predators in town, but I am hesitant. In summertime many cats are prowling and the goshawk may at any time make a highly targeted attack.

150 SPECIES OF BIRDS AMONGST THE CONCRETE

The richest areas for birds are the major natural areas beyond the city centre, but in central Stockholm you can still bird watch. In a regular year about 150 different species of birds can be seen in the inner city. Every year, there is a competition to see the most birds in town, called *Concrete Bird Watching*. Whoever spots a new species of bird in the city is given the title of *Concrete King*, gaining honour and respect.

Just like people, birds in the city are a mishmash of characters. There are the hardcore-Stockholmers (who never would move away from here) and immigrant hillbillies that ended up here on a random transit. Indeed, there are also species that commute daily between work and home.

Here are some examples of those different kinds:

The *House Sparrow* is an inveterate Stockholmer. It is a species that has become truly urban, and frankly, it would probably not survive without the city's pulse. Historically, during the 17th and 18th century, it was dependent on horse droppings to survive. Today, it is rather our waste management and the demand for fast-food upon which it thrives. Outside the densely built-up area the house sparrow would have no chance. Throughout their lives, the birds stick to the same residential area and find it difficult to expand into new areas.

A fairly new Stockholmer is the *Wood Pigeon*. A sharp migration inflow occurred in the 1980s. Until then, they had mostly bred in the surrounding forests. Nowadays, the wood pigeon is a common city bird and you can observe them build their disordered nests in window boxes and on building facades. They can also be seen in the small, scrawny trees next to the shopping areas by NK and Åhlens. It has been noticed that the mortality is greater among pigeons that nest in the cities, but they are compensated by larger litters.

A bird that many will notice is the *Barnacle Goose*. Beautiful and brave, they waddle across city lawns. They are easiest to see in Djurgården (1) and

2.

NORRMAL

WOOD PIGEON

3.

RIDDARFJÄRDEN

GOSHAWK

5.

6.

7.

ÖSTERMALM

10

9.

HOUSE SPARROW

4.

IDJURGÅRDEN

1.

BARNACLE
GOOSE

8.

ÖSTERSJÖN

SÖDERMALM

Drottningholm (2). The geese are originally from the arctic tundra, but also exist in captivity at Skansen. A few years ago some escaped and started to breed freely around Stockholm. They are now so common that authorities restrict them by culling. Although geese seem fearless, they are wild birds that migrate each fall. A few years ago there was a ringed bird on Djurgården that proved to have been born amongst the polar bears in Spitsbergen! This bird had probably met 'our' birds at wintering sites in Holland and then accompanied them for the journey north. An interesting proof that tame, released birds mix easily with wild ones.

There are also some birds that just like to stay overnight in the city. Such daily commuters are crows and gulls. In winter, they fly into Stockholm city when it starts to get dark. Several thousands of birds can sometimes gather. The ice on Riddarfjärden (3) is a traditional gathering place that has overnight protection from foxes and other predators. At dawn a big decampment strikes when the whole gang once again go out to look for food in garbage dumps and fields outside of town.

RARE VISITORS

Most bird species seen in the city have more or less involuntarily ended up here in transit. The city's location, between Lake Mälaren and the sea, causes many birds to pass through the city airspace. There are almost no limits to the species that can be seen in the sky over Stockholm. During an autumn season, one can see as many as ten different raptor species pass by, as well as flocks of thrushes, ducks and Arctic geese. These birds have no interest whatsoever in the city, they're just flying past. Sometimes if a rare bird is sighted, the alarm is sounded, and the concrete bird watchers are quick to try and get the rare birds added to the list via websites they keep track of the species seen.

WHERE TO GO BIRD WATCHING IN STOCKHOLM

In the winter many birds and bird watchers gather around the winter open water in central Stockholm. The area outside the Grand Hôtel and Kungsträdgården (4) is probably the best. Here, hundreds of mute swans hibernate. Amongst them coots, gulls, tufted ducks, mallards and mergansers flock in. The rush gets extra wild in the morning when the municipality feed the birds, a tradition that will soon be a hundred years old. And when a white-talied eagle or a goshawk suddenly appears in the sky over Gamla stan (The old town), it can get quite frenzied.

To experience the bird migration over Stockholm you suitably place yourself with patience and a good pair of binoculars on top of the city's highest point, Skinnarviksberget (**5**) in Södermalm. The most intense bird traffic fills the skies in early April mornings and again towards the end of September. As a bonus, you get a breath taking view of the city.

Summertime bird watching is probably best in one of the city's parks. The largest area is called Tantolunden-Eriksdalslunden (**6**) and it is located in Södermalm. From the promenade during the warm summer evenings, you can hear the nightingale song from Årsta holmar (**7**). To bird watch from the water is also not a bad idea. Feel free to go a place like Fjäderholmarna (**8**), known for its rich bird life. This is where the archipelago begins and it is here that you might observe species like oystercatchers, cormorants and gadwall. Otherwise, the entire island of Djurgården is very rich in birds, especially the areas around the little bird lakes Isbladskärret (**9**) and Lappkärrret (**10**) in southern and northern Djurgården.

Good luck with your bird watching, I hope you find something that may be called uncommon.

A SCENE FROM THE UNDERWORLD

TEXT: **LUDWIG SCHMITZ**

The discordant sound of rehearsal is hushed by an all-Armani dressed, pony-tailed Frenchman. It is the director (who goes by the suitable name of Jean Claude Arnault), he's come to announce that the performance is about to start. We are in a concrete basement, below a fin-de-siècle apartment building eight storeys high, where the cultural elite of Stockholm have gathered for an evening of Franz Liszt and romantic poetry, with a guest appearance of red wine in plastic cups.

The audience has already arrived down the cellar staircase. There are about a hundred people, fabricating an air of seniority, money, dignity, red wine and something else too. During the ritual of handshakes and chin kisses amongst the bohemian bourgeois, the silence suddenly cuts through their ambitions, revealing a primordial stupidity in their expressions as they concentrate to make out some sounds of surface activity.

But down here, there is no way to disturb us. Pianist Love Derwinger and soprano Barbara Hendricks begin, and a Franz Schubert Lieder vibrates between the rough, concrete walls of the cellar gallery.

Now (perhaps as someone in the left back row thinks 'aha, the allegro' and blushes with self-satisfaction) the summer heat above us reaches its climax. Thunder rumbles, rain pours through, flooding the gutters of our musical underworld with the sounds of nature. With the thunder, the rain and the Liszt fused together we stumble upon an accidental interpretation of the reverence of nature inside the music of romanticism.

In the stiff world of classical music, something like this would naturally be considered a catastrophe and its French director would, in his mind, spell out the word c-a-t-a-s-t-r-o-p-h-e. At Forum though, this is no reason to complain. If you pay the hefty price of a ticket to go down the stairs to this cellar, it's because you want something that the concert hall a few blocks away cannot offer. What that something is, well, I don't know.

Jean Claude Arnault ends the night by shaking hands with the more notable guests (but most nights this man in his late sixties, gets home in the morning, after having partied with art students and their likes). This monsieur is something of the Mephisto of the Swedish cultural scene; to the same extent hated and beloved, married to Sweden's foremost, as well as most depressed, poet (and there's a few), courting new lovers every year or so. In a country where you can't buy wine on a Saturday after 3 pm (not to speak of Sundays) that naturally goes as exciting.

Monsieur Arnault's Forum, Contemporary Scene of Culture (Sigtunagatan 14), is a product of the eighties, when Stockholm went from being the depressed, wintry place of cinematic imagination, to the minor European cultural capital of today. Twenty years ago, the Swedish artists and writers who are famous today, became so in this legendary cellar. Today it's a place where the alumni of these years gather, along with PR savvy ministers, suits, pretentious hipsters and, of course, those who happen to like classical music (and red wine).

LEAVING ÖSTERMALM

TEXT & PHOTOGRAPHY: **MATHEA SOLHEIM**

I'm sitting in my apartment with Calle, he looks like he fell out of a Ralph Lauren catalogue, he's asking if I want to join him at a rave this weekend. Rave? Is there such a thing in Stockholm? I imagine strange people wearing ugly, rustling neon clothes and buffalo shoes. It feels like an eccentric proposal.

My apartment where we sit is on Östermalmsgatan, a street that is almost two kilometres in length, stretching from Lärkstan all the way to Karlaplan. The buildings are mostly five stories high, with elegant, ornamental façades. It is a typical turn-of-the-century Östermalm apartment: high ceilings, white stucco and large windows that are south-facing. My mother decided to decorate it with contemporary chandeliers and oriental carpets. I chose several framed Mario Testino prints for the Stockholm-white walls, and that's about all I have done in this place.

My apartment is no more than five minutes away from that which is, in my opinion, the most beautiful street in Östermalm - Danderydsgatan, it's lined with cosy town houses and the Architecture School, which happens to have the reputation of being the ugliest building in Stockholm!

I feel ambivalent about Calle's idea. I don't really think it's my thing. I won't fit in there.

"Oh, come on," Calle says, "I'll sign you up, and when the weekend is here you can choose if you want to come along or not."

He types in my name and address into his *Macbook Air*.

"Don't worry, you'll love it!" he says, and gives me a pat on the shoulder.

The weekend arrives, and I've made plans with some girlfriends to meet up at Sturehof, a classic restaurant right in the heart of Stureplan. We go there

often. Usually we eat dinner in the large, well-lit dining room, where they serve traditional Swedish dishes with a French touch, or we sit at the top of Obaren, up the stairs from the dining room.

Obaren is relaxed, with dimmed lights and loud music, attracting a younger, stylish clientele. It is good to sit at the small, black table that looks towards the bar. If you feel restless, you can have a go at the Spider-Man pinball machine. Summer tends to be rather busy at Sturehof. The outdoor seating is usually crowded, we sit enjoying glasses of rosé wine and people-watching in the sun.

It's walking distance from my place, so I walk down Engelbrektsgatan then cross through Humlegården diagonally. Humlegården is a large park in central Stockholm, perfect during the day for young families and dog owners, as well as kids hanging out at the skateboard ramp. When I was at high school, we used to come here and play brännboll.

I pass the statue of Carl Linnaeus and then the Royal Library, an imposing, elegant building from the 1800s where I spent many hours before exams, then I get to Stureplan and I'm a minute away from my final destination, Sturehof.

Once inside Sturehof my cell phone rings, it's Calle. I hear his voice telling me to come to his place. My girlfriends are in the midst of a heated discussion whether V or Suite is the best 'VIP-room' at Sturecompagniet, which is three minutes away from here. Here I am with the same people, going to the same places, week in week out - even the after-parties have become routine. I ought to pull myself together. The fact that I have never even bothered to go to Södermalm is a proof that I am totally restricted. I have to go.

Calle's place is crowded with people. But these, his more alternative friends, look nothing like I had imagined ... Where are all the crazy ravers? I feel a stitch of disappointment, but I will still secretly look upon them as freaks anyway, even though really they look no different to my friends.

Calle lights up when he sees me and pours each of us a glass of wine. "Join in!" he says, "this happens only twice a year. If you don't like it, then you'll know. Then at least you tried anyway."

When the pre-ordered large cab with the direction of 'Nacka' arrives, I jump into the back seat with him. The taxi takes us out of the inner city. Turn of

the century buildings are replaced by modern buildings. I don't recognise the streets we are travelling through. I note that we cross a bridge. When we arrive, we have been driving for at least thirty minutes, or so it seems. I'm starting to doubt whether it was a good idea to join in. It's pitch black outside and we're in a desolate warehouse area, there's not a soul in sight.

"Is this really right?" I ask, sceptically. Calle nods.

"We're almost there," he says to reassure me. The rest of the gang have already started to walk towards the desolate warehouses. The taxi leaves, I'm left alone, stressed and far from home.

We walk along a deserted construction site until we arrive at the warehouse and turn into the parking lot. Now we can hear the bass, the queue is long and meandering but after a while we are let in. They make sure our names are somewhere on the list, and then we are inside. We walk down following the bass, until we arrive at a terrace where we stop and gaze out across the dance floor, teeming with all sorts of people. The music thunders. I take Calle's hot hand and he leads me gently down a steep staircase and into the great hall. I look malplacé in a short skirt, ten-centimeter heels and fur, but no one seems to care.

The décor downstairs is non-existent. What looks like a thick mattress is placed on the ground along one of the walls. It looks dirty but we sit down on it anyway. In the flashing light I observe people dancing. Sweat dripping down foreheads, eyes closed, happy faces, bodies moving in time to the music. An overwhelming sense of well-being develops, I feel as if I am one with the music.

"Do you like it?" he asks. He's sweating, as if we were sitting in a sauna. I nod.

In the taxi on the way home several hours later, through a sleepy Stockholm, I still feel elated. We now drive down Karlavägen, it's light outside, but not a soul walks the streets. I am imbued with the joy of having discovered an alternative to the rather trivial Stureplan, where you are free to do what ever you want. I can't help but smile at my prejudices, I thought that such places existed only abroad. To call it a rave wouldn't do it any justice. I mean, from what I remember, I saw no one wearing neon clothes, or those rustling pants! With so many thoughts swirling around in my head, so many new impressions, another thought appears: how nice it is to be back home in Östermalm.

STOCKHOLM PRIDE

YOU DON'T HAVE TO BE AN ABBA FAN

TEXT: **JOE DALY**

DATELINE: STOCKHOLM. 4/8/10. 10:30AM.

I was up for today's experience because it was years since I had last done it, and I was very excited – overexcited, even. We were gathered in an underground garage, somewhere in south Stockholm, in readiness for the main event when one of us would spend the day tied helplessly in a straitjacket, another bound hand and foot with leather straps to a massive, mean-looking hospital gurney. Things hadn't got off to a promising start. We had been stuck in the garage for over half an hour because no one had the code for the electronic door. Finally, a mobile rang, numbers were punched, the doors opened and out we streamed into a glorious summer morning. We were three guys, four girls and a gurney, with only half-an-hour to cross the Liljeholm road bridge and find our way deep into Tantolunden woods. Renamed Pride Park for this one week every year, Tantolunden was buzzing with fifty thousand demonstrators who, thanks to impeccable organisation in a system little short of miraculous, were seamlessly guided to their allocated slots. This was my tenth Stockholm Pride, but the first I would actually participate in, thanks to the kind invitation of KRO, the National Organisation of Artists [Konstnärernas Riksorganisation].

From its roots in Gay Pride, Stockholm Pride has matured into a demonstration sans frontières for universal equality and I, now encased in a strait jacket, was to be a proud part of it. Our group, KRO, was drawing attention to the plight of individuals in societies, past and present, where homosexuality is diagnosed as a mental illness and 'cured' by mental torture. We were lined up between Iran Solidarity's exotic belly-dancer, shaking for freedom on a flat-back truck, and the Uppsala-based members of the labour movement Vision, urging wider acceptance of lesbian, gay, bisexual and transgender people in the workplace. At one o'clock, on time and in perfect order, the parade emerged from the trees and into the glare of the sun. Showtime!

Pride week runs from Tuesday to Sunday, with Saturday the real culmination of a week when Stockholm buzzes with equality concerns fuelled by fun, so what better week to visit. The rainbow flag flies everywhere, and also on every inner city bus in a show of solidary from the Town Hall. Headquarters for the week's events is the massive public media centre, Kulturhuset, Culture House, in the centre of town. Spread over four floors and a vast roof terrace, Kulturhuset becomes Pride House for the week, filling the lecture rooms, exhibition spaces, cinema and theatre with a packed programme celebrating diversity. Children's Room and Tio Tretton, the ten to thirteen year olds' library and kitchen hangout, frees parents up to debate issues like htb refugee problems, asylum and trans-parenting in Sweden. Global sexual politics, reports from the annual World AIDS conference and, more recently, the difficulties for htb people in Russia, Eastern Europe and China have been highlighted. The significant number of influential Swedish and foreign politicians who attend clearly demonstrates the integrity and calibre of the Pride House debates.

The Pride House cinema comes into its own, while the galleries burst at the seams with work by htb artists, supplemented by equality centred exhibitions, mounted by one or another of Stockholm's major museums. Daytime offers a week's worth and more of things to see and do, and one of mine is the Wednesday afternoon Queer Tango for beginners. Held in the open-air café complex on the Pride House roof, I originally went in the hope of being swept off my feet by a passing gaucho, only to find that Queer Tango is the preserve of the ladies, the surreal factor that draws me back year after year. The ladies are very matter of fact in their approach to tango, which, as a failed student of the dance due to uncontrollable flamboyance, I think is probably a very helpful mind-set. Partners are kept at arm's length to afford a good view of the floor, passionate music sizzles in the air and the couples take tentative steps, eyes down, counting silently. An hour later, the dancers have moved in on each other, but only in the breaks in the music, but still mouthing one-two-three-and with no increase in speed. This is no Buenos Aires, but there is something nicely Nordic about the zing-free tangoistas, a smörgåsbord of check shirts and hair-gel with a hint of cats, all adding up to a lot of restrained honest fun-two-three.

For ABBA fans Pride week is paradise. You don't have to be an ABBA fan, of course, but I'd be lying if I said it doesn't help. Every club in town is geared for a week of great dance parties, but the heart of ABBA beats strong in the live shows held in Tantolunden. Wednesday night at 18.00 sees the official opening of the Pride Park main stage with its wheelchair accessible restaurants and handicap adjusted restrooms. The regular 'safe walks' back through the woods to the metro, escorted by the local residents' association, are another feather in the cap for the pride organisers. The familiar format is a welcome by a heavyweight Pride-friendly politician or two, to an evening of Swedish high camp served up by a bevy of the country's favourite singers. But on Thursday night the stars come out – it's schlagerpop night, the Europop where Abba have their roots, which traditionally sees the year's Eurovision winner gracing the Pride stage, supported by other Eurovision favourites past and present. The stage is also jumpin' on Friday and for the Saturday gala, and every night Pride Park is packed with representatives of every sexuality, joined by song.

Back to Saturday, with me immobile from the waist up, trotting docilely alongside my handsome co-victim, who was now well and truly strapped down on the gurney. The flock of white-coated psychiatrists and psychologists, made up of journalists, artists and medics, who pushed him through the streets, were headed by his eagle-eyed girlfriend. She was as satisfied he was straight as she was aware there was no curing me. Which is why I had been tied up, I figured.

In previous years I had watched the parade from further down Hornsgatan, where the crowd is always good-natured and effusive, enlivened by sports' chants backwards and forwards between the two sides of the street. I had expected this jolly crowd, but was totally unprepared for the overwhelming sincerity that crashed over us in waves of goodwill. I had always felt it, but to be a recipient of the genuine respect that filled the air was intensely moving. The normally reserved Swedes, who lined the route three and four deep, greeted us with rolls of thunderous applause and roars of encouragement and my heart swelled. That day, an estimated 500,000 people, a quarter of the municipal population, thronged the streets of Stockholm, a complete cross-section of the populace, enthusiastically clapping and cheering their encouragement for the struggle for equality for all. The proud gay police and soldiers, the proud gay teachers, students, doctors and nurses, the proud gay parents and proud parents of gay children, the proud refugees and immigrants, proud teenagers, proud golden ladies and silver foxes, proud drag queens and bears, ordinary proud transpeople and gay citizens, all of us were embraced by our peers with open hearts. The KRO statement on mental torture for homosexuals met with a truly touching response. Every year onlookers are asked to text for the group which most impressed them and, out of more than three-hundred groups, KRO was voted seventh. What a life-affirming day. Bravo Stockholm! Thank you.

ABOVE THE ESPLANADE

PHOTOGRAPHY: **EMELIE LINDGREN**

GRÖNE JÄGAREN
ALL ON RED!

LOOKING FOR AN UNCERTAIN OUTCOME

TEXT: **ALEXANDER HAVELDA**
ILLUSTRATION: **MAGDA MARNELL**

Gröne jägaren (The Green Hunter) cannot be invaded. The Green Hunter is immune. In other parts of town information reaches you and demands your attention, but here at The Green Hunter, nothing dares enter. No matter if the newspaper placards scream or not, The Green Hunter's lungs keep on pumping unevenly, eternally. Everything here is constant. When the sun pours in, through the clean spots of the windows, the venue looks like an aquarium, recently sprinkled with fish food. Once you pass the bouncer at the door, and the bouncer behind the bouncer, you leave your coat in the cloakroom. This costs 20 crowns. A bag costs 20 extra. If you try to put your coat in your bag you still have to pay 40. On your right hand side runs a bar, with men who lean upon it like a crutch.

Four nondescript beers are available on tap. A Jägermeister and a beer cost 50 crowns. A beer costs 25 before nine. After that, the price rises to 39 crowns. Walk further into the bar and you'll find the Jack Vegas slot machines, the mirrors and the toilets. There are four television screens showing sports, or shows about policemen busting dopers pushing speed limits. It smells nice, like the inside of a car. If you turn left, behind the bouncer behind the bouncer, there is a fifteen square metre room, with a broken ATM to the right and a Black Jack table to the left. The whole room is dressed in mirrors, apart from the floor, covered in a green wall-to-wall carpet, the black plastic of the carpet's spine running down the middle. During the day there is plenty of room, at night it's packed tight with people. There is no roulette table here; there's no need for it.

Behind the Black Jack table is the croupière. She is in her early twenties and hot, yet her tobacco habits have already begun to turn her skin into leather, the signs of which are most prominent around her mouth and eyes. She paces and curses, and her eyes look dead ahead. Walk further in and you'll find a large room, with seats for about sixty people and a bar to the right, with the same lame four beers on tap. Behind the bar is an Iranian guy with a finely shaped beard. He's pleasant enough but carries a self-conscious hautiness. He wears a key-chain in his trousers and speaks like Swedes do, yet more nasal. Behind him you find the menu written on black slates: Typical Swedish Plankstek 99. Filet Mignón *Black and White* 109. Nachos with salsa 49. Jägermeister and beer 50. At the end of the room there's a stage, where patrons sing karaoke in the evenings... more on this subject later.

If you exit the big room, past the room with the croupière and walk out the door, you'll find four wooden tables, just by the heavily trafficked part of Götgatan. To the left stretches the minaret, towering above the drunks in the Björns Trädgård park, in front of you lies the theatre Göta Lejon with its hipster-looking homeless wrestling in the doorway. To the right the sun projects a halo over Globen, like a spaceship over The White House. Not always of course, but that's how it was the day I got a sudden urge to put it all on red. All was thick and warm, and it was clear that something soon had to go up in smoke. Had this taken place in one of the hundred joints in Stockholm where you know beforehand in which pocket your ball will land in the spin of night - or at a place where nothing spins - there would never have been any story at all. Had she been backed up by lounge house music and daddies with curved spines and baby harnesses on their bellies, commingling with the art directors of the 2030s - magic surely would never come to be. The fact is, I went to The Green Hunter because I was looking for an uncertain outcome: for a game of social roulette. That's why everyone comes here. Despite the lack of black-red wheels, The Green Hunter is Stockholm's number one roulette venue.

THE SOCIAL ROULETTE

The day it happened I had made a date with a friend to meet around Medborgarplatsen at four, so I left my home at a quarter to. I went up the

Götgatan-hill, past teenage girls with empty cotton shopping bags, and bars promising Czech beer for 35 crowns. At the top of the hill sat a deranged man who sang a brilliant version of Morrissey's *The More You Ignore Me The Closer I Get*. As he articulated the words, he twisted his jaw: "I will creep into your thoughts like a bad debt you can't pay. Take the easy way and give in." Outside the Hotel Scandic my friend called, with unnecessary words unspoken, we decided to meet up at The Green Hunter, a hundred metres further down the road.

We drank beer after beer, as I sat with my head looking south, watching the sun transform from a halo, to kitsch, to nothing at all. When it got cold we went inside. We sat down with our backs against the wall, and soon the room went from dim to black. Someone flicked on a pair of spotlights, and in an empty second, the stage was smothered in evil, yellow light. The music was turned off, and from a corner of the room, a lonely voice announced, with part reproach, part enthusiasm, that the evening's karaoke was about to begin. The first song she sang herself; The Fugees' version of *Killing Me Softly*. She was incredibly good, and made me think of the unknown fat chick who actually sings on all of the E-type recordings, while a fit girl lip-syncing gets all the attention.

After her, a banker approached the stage to sing *Ignition* by R Kelly. After the banker, a local CIT robber preformed the theme song from *Titanic*. Both of them were great. And so was the next performer, and the next one after that. Some received applause, some didn't. Yet in the spotlight they were equally luminous. All was more, as the clock's quarters kept passing. The walls, the toilets, the roof and the knees. Fifteen lost keys, and twenty sneakers on their way to and from the bathroom. Four clocks with (Swedish beer brand) *Pripps* logos under the number 12. Pam, tick tack! Pam, tick tack! Everything, including every filthy, low-energy lamp, spat distinct sounds in perfect synch and timing. As if they all knew they were part of the evening's show. The place filled up, and the Iranian guy with the chain slid between the tables, swift as a proud ice hockey referee. The evening's social roulette had begun, and faces swam across the minutes, like butterflies in mud, silently hoping that the roulette balls would land in their empty pockets. Everyone had an almost 50 per cent chance. And everyone would have agreed on something, if the time and place were right. Not necessarily anything sexual. Just something. Half black pockets. Half red. And then a green one.

Lights were constantly blinking and eyes popped open everywhere. Every now and then a door next to the stage opened, and out came a muscular dude in an Adidas track suit, his neck densely tattooed. It was obvious that he had some kind of financial interest in the evening's turn out; turning his pit bull neck one hundred and eighty degrees, he would count the number of people in the room, then retreat back into the room behind the door. During the quiet moments in between songs, I began to hear noises from inside the room. At first I did not know if there really was a sound, or if it was the sudden silence that kept tricking my ears. After a while, however, I began to make out a repetitive sound of shock, as though coming from a lonely tool.

The quarters turned to hours, as the hours twisted heads. Stupidity and courage wrestled in the dark, under acrylic hoodies and sweaty caps with vulgar logos.

A mum of two sang about things that weren't true, while I hummed along. Then I went to the men's. By the toilet door I met a young guy in faded jeans, and two giggling teenage girls. One looked like she had just put her trousers back on, the other one chewed bubble gum and wore a jumper with the confederate flag on it. The guy held the door and greeted me with an ironic 'welcome', followed by intense girlish giggling. It was cool, but I got nervous and felt unsexy. Clumsy. I went back to my table, sat down next to my friend, and engaged intensely and sincerely, in a perfect dialogue in which he couldn't hear me and I was deafened by the sound of my own voice. The dark door next to the stage opened more frequently, the focused counting man would emerge each time with a look that mattered, repeat the hundred and eighty turn, count and retreat. When I saw him for the fourth time, a song had just faded out. The sounds behind the open door were as clear as a personal attack alarm from the pocket of a lonely blonde. I heard four or five barks, before the door shut. This made me leave the room once more, this time for a smoke.

Outside the main entrance, Stockholm hanged in a thin snare between Saturday night and Sunday morning. Vulture-like pirate taxi drivers repeated their tired mantra: "Taxi?" " Taxi?" "Taxi?" some drunk answered "Bus?" to the delight of every middle class hero that happened to be around. Warm smoke rose from young, chattering mouths to quietly dissolve into the light-dark sky. Twenty girls picked up twenty scarves from twenty cloth bags. Pimple-scarred, beady-eyed boys faked grim, as if just having received the unfortunate news that a giant rock once again had to be rolled up the hill before dawn. Soon there would be disappointment for most, and evil, perverse destructive fantasies coming true for a few lucky ones. Globen was soon to resurrect. I watched the vultures circling, following those who have strayed too far, or those who do not realise how far they still have to go, at the end of the night their undisputed first choice are the presumptuous winners of the gamble, and the unsound ones who have nothing left to lose. "How much to Fruängen?" " – 250" " – fuck no!" " – 200!" "OK, let's go!" Slow engine. A u-turn. Then sail away to the south. Or north. To spaces between bedside tables.

ALL ON RED!

After I finished my cigarette and returned to my seat, two or three appearances followed that I hardly registered. Then the very thing occurred, a moment which rose above the night, and somehow still is hanging, like a black cloud above my head. What was it then that left such traces behind my eyes that I, out of all the places in Stockholm, choose to tell you about the Green Hunter? A beautiful girl approached the stage to sing. Nothing more. Everyone has a trigger, which sooner or later makes them join in the Green Hunter madness roulette. It might be the karaoke, the mirrors, or a sweater with the flag of the confederation. For me it was her. She entered, and suddenly it became impossible for me to continue the role as one of the evening's spectators. Because of her, I obsessively wanted to see the colours spin. I felt an urge to let the roulette stew boil all the black and the red in to a filthy mush, and let my mind repeatedly whisper *red, red, red* – I had suddenly put it all on red!

The intro to Jay-Z's *Empire State of Mind* tumbled out of the speakers as she raised the mic to her lips. Then silence. The toxins had turned my body into a balloon. All was on hold. The wheel was spinning! A woman among apes. My thoughts fluttered, as a pathetic slow-mo feeling intensely took over my mind.

I had to win her over. She left the stage and the ball whirled in my skull for an eternity without ever touching ground. A real estate broker went up on stage and sang Cher's *If I Could Turn Back Time*. I was numb. I was all in. What could I lose? I pretended to go to the bathroom again, to look for her. I checked the bars, by the Jack Vegas slot machines, by the bathroom and the bouncers. Nowhere. I went out and by the first step on the sidewalk, the panicked wheel inside my forehead got jammed in a sudden final spasm: I saw her. The ball was jumping! It slowed down. I saw her. Not alone. I recognized his lips - the *Focused Counter* guy! Green pocket! End of play. What were the odds?

She talked to the bouncer, then said goodbye. The Focused Counter zipped up his track suit. The two of them got into a taxi and a vulture slammed the door behind them. Then away. A new round. New players. Not me. I went back to my table and the space in my head, where the ball of pathetic hope had clattered just a moment ago, was now filled up with pubertal thoughts of loss. How the fuck could I be that dumb? Why gamble? For the hope of bragging and forgetting? Or the actual enjoyment the prize could have given? That's how new generations of gamblers are born. From time to time, fathers leave their offices in the middle of the day, and when they return cake is being served. Winners do exist. That is true. But all winnings are, sooner or later, squandered. That's why one should never gamble. At the end, all will be worn out. She. *Focused Counter*. Me.

If I Could Turn Back Time faded out and the real estate broker remained on the quiet stage with his feet straddled wide apart, and one fist raised in the air. In the spotlight he looked like a cross between a glam rocker and Jessie Owens. The whole venue was blinking in green and black, and from behind the black door came the sound of a barking dog.

94

VÄRMDÖ

TEXT: **KARIN STRÖM**
PHOTOGRAPH: **HELGE STRÖM**

There's a hierarchy within the different islands in the Stockholm archipelago. The further from the mainland, the higher the status they enjoy. People inhabiting the outer islands, which often can be reached only by boat, scoff at those inhabiting the inner, insinuating that this is not the real archipelago. Värmdö is probably quite far down these peoples' list. It's an enormous island – the fifth biggest in Sweden, directly adjacent to Stockholm and linked to the city by the bridge Skurusundsbron. Personally I like going to Värmdö by car or bus. I love the brutality of the six-lane motorway blazing through the grandiose landscape of water, cliffs and small houses seen from far away.

The closest you come to a town on Värmdö is Gustavsberg, named after the 1600th century politician Gustaf Oxenstierna who owned an estate nearby. While the centre – easily reached from central Stockholm by a 25-minute bus ride – is not much more than a shopping mall, a pizzeria, a food store and a healthcare centre, the harbour is home to Gustavsbergs Porslinsfabrik, Sweden's last remaining porcelain factory. Founded in 1825, it had a major impact on the development of Gustavsberg, which soon became a model factory town dominated by various progressive owners. (Due to the good conditions that the workers were offered, they didn't form their own labour union until almost a generation later than the rest of Sweden.) With renowned ceramics designer Stig Lindberg as head designer the factory became one of Sweden's most influential design institutions during the 1900's, literary churning out classics. Today the factory features a museum with company history alongside contemporary ceramics exhibitions. A more recent addition to Gustavsberg's cultural supply is Artipelag, a massive contemporary art gallery founded and financed by Björn Jakobsson, more known as the brain behind the baby carrier Baby Björn. As a great lover of both art and nature, Björn chose to locate his wonderfully megalomaniac exhibition hall at Hålludden among rocks, cliffs, pine trees and spruces, complete with two restaurants and a museum shop (full of baby stuff).

Both Gustavsbergs Porslinsfabrik and Artipelag are easily reached by bus from Stockholm, but for the nature buff that wants to see more of the actual island, exploring it by bike is probably the best option. Värmdö has an infinite number of small straits, coves, capes and peninsulas and the best way to find your own favourite is to bike wherever the road takes you. In July, the small beaches get packed with people from the increasing number of all-year-round residents, but the rest of the summer months it's mostly just compact silence only disturbed by the random boat chugging by – perfect for skinny-dipping. And whenever you get tired of island life, just peddle back to the city. To me that's the archipelago at its best, whatever those snobs of the outer islands might say.

COLD FEET

TEXT & PHOTOGRAPHY: **SIMON SKUTELI**

There he stood, with his toes right on the edge, knees slightly bent and the upper part of his body leaning forward, like an S or a ⵒ, depending on which way you saw him from. The towel lay neatly folded on the cliff and the socks were tucked into his shoes. The rest of his clothes were put in his rucksack, inside a plastic bag, to protect them against splashes and drops. In the rucksack were also keys to his home, a mobile phone in protective case, an almost new notebook, two functioning pens and a wallet in brown leather. In the wallet were two hundred kronor notes, eighteen kronor in coins, a dozen plastic cards for different uses, a good bunch of receipts of which the oldest was one year and four months, two condoms, two plasters and a four-leaved clover sticker – a gift from a person whom he didn't actually know that well.

Before him a few mosquitoes buzzed in tight circles, without any attempt to attack him, possibly only interested in the heat radiating from his body. The air was significantly cooler than during the day and small shivers were going through the skin of his naked arms and legs. But what really made him shiver was not the temperature of the air, but rather, the thought of the cold water.

Did anyone force him to jump into the lake?

No

Was he in company with a group of bathing enthusiasts, before whom he didn't want to seem sensitive? Was he obsessed or did he have masochistic feelings towards life? No, but he had certain conceptions, of how it looked, when I swam, when the water licked his blond hair over his brow and down his cheeks, when the lips' concentrated breathing inhaled the oxygen merely millimetres above the water surface, when his pale body went off like a missile between the swim strokes and became one with the wet, black silence.

Exhale
listen
look at the view

There he stood, with his toes by the edge, with his hip and head on opposite sides of the vertical axis, so that the balance could easily be controlled by the help of the feet. Like an upside-down pendulum the body imperceptibly circulated around its centre of gravity, compensating any hint of motion with a slight displacement in the opposite direction. The brain's unconscious calculations were even and the sum was his balance. Meanwhile, the conscious part of the brain was occupied by the horror, the horror of the displacement, before the almost unnoticeable change that would result in the strong sensation of cold. The transition from the body's safe oscillating to the accelerating movement that would lead him into the water, he would perceive too late, he knew. When the movement would be obvious enough for the mind to get a hold of it there would be no way to turn back. At the same time, it was into the water he wanted – to be embraced by the liquid darkness, to see his fingers cut through the surface – but the cold... If there only had been a ladder.

From a jetty a bit further away excited shouts and the sound of lapping waves was heard. Last one in, he thought, but remained in place on the cliff. With his hands he made some swimming stroke-like movements in the air. Slowly, he stretched out his arms in front of him and then pulled them back behind his shoulders, and one could get the impression that he was practicing for something complicated or was warming up the joints. Was it really his decision that would be the cause? Was it on his own initiative he would release the balance and

precipitate himself towards the reflection of the sky, didn't it just happen? But if
that was the case, was it then not he whom had taken the bike out of the rack and
pedalled here, was it not he whom had packed the bathing-trunks in the bag?
He tried to remember how he had handled similar situations in the past, what he
used to think of during that second between the ledge and the water surface, or
the second before. Were there any words, was he a thinking being?

And convulsions
yes
in the stomach
the chest and
the legs

inhale
wait

VAGRANT IN A STRANGE LAND

PRELIMINARIES FOR FURTHER EXPLORATION OF STOCKHOLM

TEXT: **MATTIAS FORSHAGE**

This city is what it appears to be, and not. It is a jungle, a vast wasteland, a doll's house, a prison, a crowded yet empty arena, a forest of symbols. It is a *reasonable space for living*. For some of us Stockholm forms the surroundings, is that *spatial given*. No less than the temporary visitor do we need to discover and co-create it. It depends on us to do it. Otherwise we would allow it to be merely the utterly dull, functional background of repetitive habits, or the props for a touristic commercial. It needs to be appropriated, played with.

Isn't there quite often a space just next to the main route, which is all unused and quite still, where litter amasses? But is it really entirely unused? Who strays from the paths in major parklands such as Djurgården, and what is to be found by doing that? When does the urge to go strolling in the Frihamnen harbour arise? Under what circumstances do we dare explore narrow spaces between large buildings and steep rocks?

Much of the total area of this city is taken up by larger parks, and the official pathways through them are few, so what is there along the unprotected borders and in the hidden spots? Who goes there and what do they leave behind? What does that say about the city as a place for living?

But let's try to situate it objectively first. Stockholm takes place in an overlap between zones or categories. It is coastal but not maritime, it is at the crossroads of southern nemoral habitats and northern boreal habitats (typically with northern coniferous forest on northern slopes or poor soils, southern deciduous forest on southern slopes or rich soils), it is geologically very old (the bedrock)

102

but recently risen out of the sea; it fulfills all criteria of being fully urban, slightly cosmopolitan, yet not very crowded, cosy, and easy to cross on foot; the population is heterogeneous and there are very few fractions large or stubborn enough to maintain distinct communities or subcultures that might control neighbourhoods.

There is the usual precarious ecological situation: massive consumption of resources demanding vast hinterlands (near or far) to produce the goods needed and to deal with the waste produced. There are the usual contrasts between silent homesteads for the wealthy and lively or even noisy residential areas for others, between areas that are rigorously designed, controlled or cleaned and those that are subject to spontaneous transformation, uncontrolled use, decay and growth; and between economically intense commercial sites where everything is designed to facilitate consumption (and to clearly suggest that anything beside paid consumption is illegitimate) and on the other hand backwaters, backyards, hinterlands, interspaces, unexposed corners, and abandoned sites; between old and new; between rich and poor; between natural conditions and artificial; between human intentions and the more or less uncontrollable interests of other species; vegetation, birds, insects; between the imposed order of work/consumption and the very mixed real desires of the human inhabitants.

All such contrasts provide a favourable setting for an active exploration of the urban environment as a living space, of what we might call an active geography. We go hunting, we abandon, we go astray, we go on a quest, we get lost, we find.

We can just continue enumerating questions, still mere examples, restricted to the more modest ones: Why are there so distinct atmospheres in certain neighbourhoods which are just slightly separated from the surroundings? And what are the consequences of intentional isolation (like the neighbourhood Atlasområdet)? Why are some little squares always empty? What plants, animals, people colonise newly created spaces, and with what adaptations? Specifically when do the hidden little parks of Hälsingehöjden and Bjurholmsplan, or the marginal parks on the outskirts of the inner city, such as Fredhällsparken and Eriksdalslunden, reveal themselves to the wanderer? And especially the vast space under bridges! What could actually be done there? Or a more extended under-bridge-type space like Järnvägsparken? And who has even noticed the bus terminal that was never taken into use on top of the Gamla Stan metro station? When is the end of the road actually the end of the road?

It is easy to go walking in Stockholm. Alone or in a group, by night or by day, in summer or in winter, with empty pockets, or carrying equipment for documentation and investigation. The topography is variable, and even more so the ambient topography; the distribution of ambiances, the flow of attractions and repulsions, the psychogeographical landscape. In Stockholm, the physical obstacles for continuing in a direction are in fact more often natural barriers like waterlines or steep rock sides rather than artefactual ones such as highways, railways and fences. In Stockholm, the public transport system is omnipresent and efficient; wherever you end up, there is usually a comfortable way to return from there. In Stockholm, there is still a low level of violence, so it remains relatively safe to walk alone. It is not untrue as many visitors say, that the Swedes are generally shy and distance-maintaining but polite, helpful and even very sociable once someone else takes the initiative and the ice is broken; this means that strange behaviours (as active space investigation will often encompass) usually will go undisturbed, though passers-by can be approached for help.

Indeed, taking a random walk, 'drifting', is a geographical experiment, an enterprise in revealing the latent structure of the city. Taking a random walk is also a poem. There will be a complex interaction between reveries, desires and on going psychic conflicts and adventures on the one hand, and all those elements encountered on the walk on the other hand: all the random meetings with acquaintances and strangers, random objects lying around, random messages, street-signs, posters, shop windows, garbage, lost objects. Encounters provide answers and questions, the vigilant yet selective attentiveness of thought focuses on things that take part in current chains of associations, trains of thoughts, complexes of concepts, and do that very often just ahead of conscious thought, providing striking chance encounters; things reveal or acquire meaning. Sometimes drifting may lead to a dramatic chain of events, to the striking clusters of meaning sometimes referred to as 'objective chance', and to a sense of re-enchantment. But also where such exaltation does not occur, there will always be meaningful patterns, loads of data, poetic elements, corrections and provocations in terms of reflection and introspection.

Some parks, some little squares, some bridges, some old buildings, some dead ends, will prove to be strangely recurring. Popular use will prove to deviate from that intended by city planners. There will be peeking behind the given outlines, there will be trespassing. A lot of interspaces, hidden corners and abandoned spots will emerge in the middle of seemingly well-known neighbourhoods; they were there all the time but remained somehow invisible as long as orientation was subjected to practical concerns.

If the random walk seems light-hearted, more ambitious experiments can easily be designed. Throwing darts on a map. Trying to follow a map of another city. Systematically investigating spots that look mysterious on the map. Systematically following trails of association among street names and place names. Looking for previous, overbuilt layers of city planning or of topography. Following suggestions in dreams and random associations. Following random sets of instructions devised by others.

All of this will show another face of the city, and of life. The explorative part of reconquering our living space for our own individual and collective desires. Reclaiming the city. A somnambulist treasure hunt. Surrealists have always been walking a lot, often random walking, acknowledging the lattice of meanings gradually revealed, fascinated by the phenomenology of the urban, stubbornly connecting it with poetic phenomenology, ludic methodology and imagination. In the mid-90s the surrealist group in Stockholm conducted a series of investigations into what was then referred to as the 'atoposes' or 'worthless places' of Stockholm. We gradually converged onto a classification of them (based on genesis and main characteristics), devised schemas to characterise them and to detail their flora which is highly significant. Certain suggestions were further developed in other kinds of surrealist games.

We did particular investigations of randomly picked parts of the city. Easternmost Kungsholmen, very inner city but crammed with small spots of different atmospheres. There, at Kungsklippan, we followed hidden tunnels in the shrubs to secret dens, we enjoyed the desolateness of carpet-beating spots, we populated the blind corners of semi-abandoned stairs and carefully listed all the plants we could find there, we collected weird artefacts, we set out for trajectories in the shade of walls and we allowed gravity to lead us to secluded spots of accumulation. We analysed, adjusting our categories, understanding the dynamics of abandonment and reclaiming.

Another example: the Gärdet area, with less spatial restrictions and thus larger forgotten areas, industrial-area-type ruderal spaces, variable park land - a suburban feeling. Even Gamla Stan was a rewarding exploration, despite it being so small, crammed and adapted to tourists. Worthless places are everywhere, they are ever-changing, there is a constant movement of drifting in and out of use, rebuilding and decaying, tidying and abandoning.

The urban landscape is forever mutating, everything remains to be discovered. As the unknown is inexhaustible our struggles, be they introspective, artistic, quasi-scientific or actually scientific, will merely tap into successive layers of open or hidden meanings. New detours branch off, new fields of possibilities and frameworks of meaning consolidate. New future conflicts and future revelations stand there waiting to be encountered.

FURTHER READING:
Additional theorising and documentation of these and similar investigations can be found in:

(In English) M Forshage: "Worthless places", M Forshage & Erik Bohman: "Towards the Solidification and Relativisation of Atopos Theory", and various other items on <www.icecrawler.com>, in the surrealist journal *Phosphor* (Leeds) 2008- , and in the anthologies *Hydrolith* 2010 and *The Exteriority Crisis* (eds Jacobs, Bragg, Castro) 2009.

(In Swedish only) M Forshage: "Lyckans politik", in *Autistisk Kilskrift*, Stockholm 2006, Per Sigurd Lindberg: *Stockholmsfloran*, Stockholm 1983; *Stora Saltet* 1995-98 (especially issues #2 "Geografi" and #7 "Upphittat").

A NIGHT AT SÖDRA TEATERN

TEXT & PHOTOGRAPHY: **BILLIE LINDAHL**

On this particular night, quite unusually, there are many people running around, trying to make everything work. They are on the stairs with their walkie-talkies, in the cellar loading gear, in the doorways receiving tickets, behind the bars taking orders. While the lobby is filling up with people, chatting over sparkling wine, we are occupying the backstage room, tuning instruments, practising songs. This night there is a film festival at *Södra Teatern* in Stockholm, and I am playing with my band *Promise and the Monster*.

Södra Teatern is a large, yellow building, standing on a solid rock face that drops towards the sea at Stadsgården. If you were to stand down there, with your back against the harbour and your eyes toward the hillside, you would view something like a giant shelf, full of bric-a-brac: dirty, neon commercials, worn out facades, protruding poles, old brick chimneys, withered stairs. From that position, the theatre, with its shiny, golden letters on the front, and the carefully polished exterior, looks otherworldly. And if you were to walk the winding cobblestone stairs up to the entrance of the building and enter, you would discover that once inside its belly, it is easy to get lost. There are so many hallways and doors, rooms and passages.

The theatre had its grand opening in 1852, and for a few years prospered as a scene for cabarets and vaudevilles. The road ahead would then become rougher. The building burned down in 1857, but was later rebuilt. In 1873 it ran out of money, which led to the head director shooting himself in the attic (the story goes that his ghost still walks around up there). In 1896 the prohibition of alcohol caused the audience to flee. Finally, in 1958, it was decided that *Södra Teatern* would be demolished. It almost happened, but after protests, and by some luck, the theatre survived. Today it is established as one of Stockholm's most versatile and thriving spots for music and the arts. It is host to festivals, burlesque clubs, and lectures; there are shows with punk bands, folk artists and electro acts. I have attended concerts there since I was a kid, and I love to play there, because of the history, and because of the building itself.

This particular night however, turns out to be quite odd. When it is decided that we are going to play on the main stage, after a long documentary film, we anticipate a disastrous show. The optimal audience is not one that has been watching slow and shaky clips for two hours before your set. When the film is over we hear a thundering applause in the speakers, and we start to walk toward the stage. Down the stairs, through a long corridor, up the other stairs, and into the black vastness, we sit down on our chairs behind the big film screen, and it rises in front of us. The concert hall is as beautiful as always, with its crystal chandeliers and ornaments in gold on the ceiling. It is also, as we suspected, totally empty. The bar has called.

RECREATE

THE WINTERS HELP ME DREAM

ILLUSTRATION: **JOHAN BARRETT**

MID CENTURY BOATING LIFE

THREE VILLAGES ON THE ISLAND OF MÖJA 1942-65

TEXT: **ERIK NORDLANDER**
PHOTOGRAPHY: **KAI GULLBERG**

LÅNGVIK 1942

May 1st 1942, my grandmother's family take the Waxholm ferry to Långvik on the island of Möja, in search of a summerhouse. They decide to rent a little cottage from a woman who will come to be known as aunt Olga. In the following summers of '43, '44 and '45 they rent the same house, then they move into the bottom floor of aunt Olga's main house. Olga moves up a floor to live upstairs during the summer.

Olga grows strawberries on the island of Norrö, north of Möja. She knows everything about growing strawberries. The strawberry harvest lasts for one month during the summer, starting around the midsummer holiday. My grandmother partakes in picking strawberries on Norrö. The remuneration at the time is 5 öre per litre. You get tanned calves and backs when picking strawberries. One litre costs 1 kroner and 10 öre to buy. So when my grandmother has picked 22 litres she brings one litre back home!

LÖKA 1956-60

My grandmother, my grandfather, my mother and her older sister rent the bottom floor in the yellow tower villa for the summer of '56 and onwards. They enjoy a good view over the harbour. On the upper floor lives a woman with her three sons; they play cards to decide who's doing the washing up duty.

1957, my grandparents buy the wooden boat, Solön, for 6,000 kronor on the advice of my grandmother's mother. They sell the previous boat *Wallkaian*.

The family rent a red two-storey house from one of the islanders. From the house they enjoy a wide view of the sea, north of Möja. The owner lives in the kitchen during the winter and moves out to a shack during the summer when the family moves in. My mother's older sister plays hide and seek with friends down in the village. Once in a while my mother is permitted to participate in the game.

After the many summers spent on the island of Möja, my family sold the wooden boat, bought a fiberglass sailboat and moved on to buy a house on a neighbouring island.

SAMI SAMI, BUT DIFFERENT

MAGDA MARNELL
ALEXANDER HAVELDA

Just like most Stockholmers, I don't really have my roots here.

My great aunt Vivan was born in 1910 in Kiruna, above the Arctic Circle.

She lived there until she was 25. Until then she had never experienced daylight during winter, nor a summer sun down.

For kicks, she and her siblings decided to move to Stockholm, which at that time was like moving from Stockholm to Jupiter today.

In the capital, people found her fascinating, and pretty soon she got a job as a native Swedish Sami, at the city zoo Skansen. Next to the bears, the wolves and the elks, she lived there in front of visitors' staring eyes.

One day King Gustav visited her, together with the King of Siam.

Another time she and her Sami family were interviewed on Sweden's biggest (and only) TV show.

When she died her family stayed on in Stockholm.

She never told anyone that she wasn't really a Sami.

VIVAN AND HER WHOLE FAKE SAMI FAMILY VISITING THE TV SHOW HYLANDS HÖRNA IN THE 1950S. (MY GRANDFATHER TOOK A PHOTO OF THE TELEVISION).

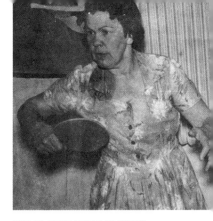

GREAT AUNT VIVAN PLAYING
TABLE TENNIS.

VIVANS GRAND DAUGTHER YLVA AS A SAMI
AT SKANSEN..

ME AND MY GRANDMOTHER
IN THE EARLY '80S.

BRÄNNBOLL

TEXT & PHOTOGRAPHY: **DEA SARACEVIC**

HOW TO PLAY:

You need some friends.

You can play it almost anywhere in Stockholm, the only thing you need is an adequate grass plot and equipment to get the game started.

A few recommended golden spots:

Gärdet (open-field).

Djurgården (royal and lush).

Hagaparken (favourite park in Stockholm).

Rålambshovsparken (flat, inner-city vibe with lots of people hanging around).

The good thing about Brännboll is that you can be dressed however you want. Preferably bring some food and drinks for a good feeling, and to hopefully celebrate your victory later on.

RULES:

The game consists of two teams that take turns on being the 'IN' and 'OUT' team. The IN team's mission is to hit the tennis ball with a bat and then try to run as far as they can. Hopefully you can run the whole way around the marked area and collect points for each member that gets back to the cue. If the OUT team catches the ball while you are still running it's called a 'lyra', and if the catcher even grabs the ball and yells "BURNED" you have to go back to where you started and the OUT team gets one point.

So, basically don't run if you see that your hit is not strong enough (but of course be brave - occasionally).

If you're part of the OUT team you collect points by catching the ball. You get more points if you manage to do it with one hand. So try it but be careful because it can easily bounce on the palm of your hand, and then your team mates will be a bit moody for losing points.

RAIN-FREE WEATHER
AND A BIT OF NORDIC LIGHT
FOR THE LATE NIGHT PLAYERS.

STUFF YOU MA

BATS
· THE FLAT (THE EASY TO HIT, NOT SO FAR RUN)
· THE ROUND (THE HARD TO HIT, VERY FAR)

TORÖ STENSTRAND

TEXT & PHOTOGRAPHY: **INKA & NICLAS**

We found Torö beach three years ago, our work at that time was dealing with the psychological effects of different nature phenomena and elements. We had just taken an interest in the meditative and spell-binding qualities of the horizon, and we were looking for a nice scene to start off from. Although the Stockholm archipelago is magnificent, all those islands obstruct the view and we had some trouble finding a spotless, clean horizon within a fair distance.

After consulting some friends who own boats, we found it. Just one hour drive south towards Nynäshamn was where that razor sharp horizon and pink sunset sky would be. The beautiful pebbled beach at Torö is typically where the Stockholm surf and kite surf crowd go, when the conditions are right. For us it has become a spot we come back to again and again to work, or just to let the ocean help us figure out what to do next.

Bring a jacket.

SAGA XIII

SAGA XIV

FROM BJÖRNS
TRÄDGÅRD TO RÅLIS

PHOTOGRAPHY: **JIMMY CROONA**

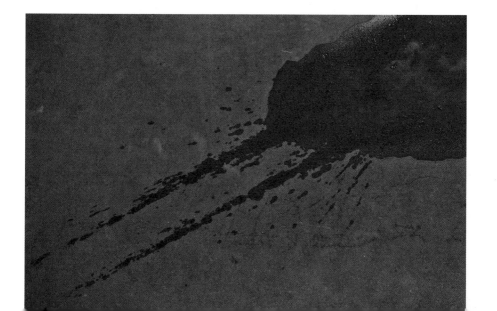

DOG ABOUT TOWN

TEXT: **OSCAR CARLSON**
PHOTOGRAPHY: **MÄRTA THISNER**

When I finally got out in the morning, the first thing I noticed was that someone unfamiliar had passed me by. Across the street from our entrance, there is an electric circuit box that also acts as the central point for organic memos posted by the canine community of Birkastan. Someone, some body, had minutes earlier passed this very spot and it was an unfamiliar body. Who is this, I wondered? One thing I was sure of was that the mark told of someone who was in the business to deliver a message of arrival to the community, but without making any other statement than that. Very elegant, I thought. What's more, this was not just some regular visitor; this fine lady was here to stay.

I was getting to the more intricate parts of the presentation when I was violently pulled at my neck and reminded to continue carrying out my morning business. My owner's enthusiasm for snow had waned steadily since winter's sudden manifestation a week ago and was trying to get me to hurry up. I on the other hand could not get enough of this stuff. It freshened everything up, helped me visually to navigate hotspots and best of all, the joy of just rolling around in it. There had been no major events since my last walk, Roxy seemed to be coming down with some infection so I figured I would stay away from her but then again, her kind is not really suitable for this climate, standing on three legs in October, come on!

On the way back I kept the pace nicely so that I could stop and see if I could get anything more out of what this stranger was trying to convey. This strategy did not work and I was again exposed to the strangling effect of the leash but I

did everything in my power to get a hint more out of the yellow infusion. I had not come across this one anywhere else on my regular short routine and was keen to find out more, to say the least.

After my owner unleashed me in the house I ran straight through the hallway into the reception room where a sofa, so deep no person could sit properly in, acted as a ramp for my surface to air ascent toward the windowpane. I turned my body mid air so that I wouldn't turn into a Boston terrier. With a loud thud I hit the window but landed safe on all four. I stood still waiting for a reaction, which arrived as a surprised look on the face of my owner.

I sat down, looking out the window and hoped for a permit to stay. I was left to continue my surveillance over the spot where I had noticed the eloquent stranger markings. I had been using this windowpane, facing the street, many times before but only when I've been left alone. It is ideal for lookout but I'm not sure it is OK for me to be up there. I took a chance this time as I deemed it necessary and it seemed to have left my owner puzzled but not too anxious. By looking out the window it must have been obvious that's what I wanted to do, which was no lie.

No one of interest passed the spot, only familiar faces and asses. Along came Astor, gushing his urine all over the place in his usual sloppy style. I knew it would be difficult to make out the scent of my interest in that mess. But the smell had already made quite an impression I was sure wouldn't go away easily. And Astor would hardly qualify as a competitor, the deaf and half-blind son-of-a-bitch he is. Well, at least I'm not deaf and half-blind.

Feeding was announced in the kitchen for the second time and I had better make my way in there, otherwise I might encounter problems in being allowed back on the windowpane. Only by showing independence and responsibility one can stretch one's allowances and gain the trust of the people who think they run your life. The food was presented and thankfully it was no different from any other meals. I thought even less of what it was and washed it down a couple of gulps of water as I intended to make my way straight back to the windowpane. From the hallway I increased the speed and made for the sofa when I saw movement in the corner of my right eye. The kid came into the reception room from the other door and I had already made my leap from the floor that would take me to the leg resting area, which would form a base for the second leap. The aborted triple jump resulted in a crash that looked much nastier that it actually was. This was much thanks to the cushions and the fact that I was partly bred to dive fearlessly into piles of rocks to chase rodents. The kid stood still and when she opened her mouth and started turning her head I let out a little cough, which successfully called off her alarm. I sat nicely, looking at her while panting happily. She ran up to me giving me strokes and hugs and asked if I was all right. I licked her face that was slathered with the foul taste of salty caviar. Astor's urine would be a blessing.

I did perhaps not have another chance at finding myself on the windowpane again today because I did not want to risk a ban of this excellent lookout post by exposing the access stunt. They would then definitely move the couch, as happened with chaise-lounge in front of the fireplace. There would be plenty of occasions for keeping an eye on the electric box on the street.

The morning proceeded as usual and I was summoned to the hallway, as we were about to embark on the daily trip to the Dog Cave. As soon as we got out of the entrance I pulled and pulled toward the box spot where I was met by an unwelcoming haze suspended in the air, which was that of Astor's visit fifteen minutes earlier. I couldn't make out if she had been by the box again, even if she did slip by without my notice.

Usually, the politics of the logistics are that I am being taken to the Dog Cave. Not that I reluctantly go, on the contrary, I love this place. But today I did the pulling of the leash. My owner was clearly having difficulties making forward in the snow, made worse by my pulling. The sidewalks are usually the last to get the snow cleared. In sub zero temperatures, the snow mixes up with salt and gravel to create a cookie dough-like substance, difficult to walk in if you've only got two feet. We, or I, turned on Karlbergsvägen and headed straight for the Dog Cave, passing Günter's hot dog kiosk where I usually stop hoping for a miracle that never happens. My owner did not say a word however. He did have a concerned look on his face though. But what could I have done, I was preoccupied to say the least.

It was as if the scent of this lady had set up shop in my olfactory area, my nose was in wide-scanning mode, which worked pretty much like the mouth of a whale. Or not really but vast amount of information was filtered through it. If the nose is set on centre focus, that meatball on the moon is mine but it was the wide scanning of the street that brought me a fresh mark. She had been here too. I made off across the street with my owner dropping the leash in chock. There were not any cars to dodge and my owner was again struggling to climb over the ridge of snow that lined all the streets in Stockholm. Without difficulties I myself arrived at a section of an cast iron fence, behind a bus shelter. I inhaled a tropical forest, a secret beach in Thailand and the peak of an alp that sees the sunrise hours before the valley beneath. The scent of this bitch had infinite nuances. My eyes were closed and nostrils wide open, the racket I heard but ignored behind me materialized in a dramatic blow to my neck and an actual flight through the air. I landed on my back but quickly spun back on all four. I was in trouble. The words that came out of my owner's mouth were a saga of anger and threats. I curled my head to look cute but it didn't really work. My behaviour was truly unacceptable, I am the first to agree, I had exposed both my owner and myself to a great deal of danger. I knew I had a long period of good behaviour ahead of me. Some people say that dogs don't come back from the vet after a few incidents of bad behaviour and I do not want to test the truth in this matter.

The remaining walk to the Dog Cave was not long and I strutted as if in a show next to my owner. He was still muttering to himself when we arrived but during the walk I went over the pieces of information that I had. The female dog of interest had exposed a number of new qualities in the liquid dossier left behind the bus shelter. It showed a great deal of discretion to use the bus shelter as protection against invasive looks. This is probably a continental habit and nothing short of extraordinary. She must definitely come from a metropolis of some kind. There were also traces of an upbringing in a home with restrained excess. She hadn't been fed the nicest cuts even though they were around, and that indicates an upbringing resulting in good manners and discipline. One can always tell if someone is carrying swag or elegance by the distribution of urine. This one spoke of delicate movements and where graciousness was in perfect balance with efficiency. It reminded me of a Japanese tea ceremony.

I was greeted by the usual tantrums from the hoodlums with the doldrums. They were kept in the deepest corner of this sub-street level dog day-care establishment called the Dog Cave. Distributed over a thin, elongated floor plan were six rooms or divisions. It gave the impression of submarine. In each room there was a pack of four to eight dogs, chosen by temper, size and sex. All of us agree that this is ridiculous. As if we couldn't deal with it ourselves. The first thing I did was to call out to Astor that he'd better remove the sprinkler system from his ass. Remembering that he is near deaf I regretted having publicly insulted him but the damage was already done. My comment was however met with laughter from all six cells. My owner was clearly still upset when he left and I felt bad. There had been an influx of emotional turmoil this morning. I better have a rest and as soon as I was let into my cell I leaped up on to the sofa and cuddled up to the reader. Each cell has a person spending time with the dogs. Well, we do as we please really and don't mind this person too much as they mostly sit, read, and study. But quite often they scratch you behind the ear. Our reader is particularly good at this but then I haven't had the opportunity to be scratched by any of the other ones since we never physically interact with them or any of the dogs in the other groups. We have our other ways, our own ways.

Everyone has appeared and soon there is a fog-like calm hovering in the Dog Cave. The morning news and gossip had been exchanged and everyone was at ease in their spot and generally content. This was when I heard the street-level door open and a pair of steps coming down the concrete stairs. The person with two legs wore some very high heels and I could tell that it was someone used to wearing them as the pace was kept fearlessly in the extremely steep staircase. Everyone having gone down that stairwell will forever show respect for it. It is notorious for causing back problems and dachshunds must be carried. Already impressed with the human, I then heard the four-legged creature stride down the stair in a fashion reminiscent of ballet. No one has ever dealt with that staircase in this way. I put two and two together when I realized something; she was here.

As if I had been lying on a landmine that suddenly went off, I flew through the air and ran for the metal mesh gate that made up the partition to our room. The others looked at each other but kept quiet. They were obviously under the impression that someone new had arrived but I could tell that it was only I that knew who it was. Trying to get a glimpse of the corridor is difficult due to its extreme angle. However, the scent came dancing and swaying through the air. I could almost see it and as the vaporized dream hit my nostrils, my hopes were confirmed. I couldn't quite believe that she had materialized here in the Dog Cave but it made perfect sense when I thought about it. She had been on her morning walk just before I did so that is why I got the fresh mark she left on the electric circuit box announcing her arrival but saying no more than that. Good skills in diplomacy. Then the mark behind the bus shelter must mean it is part of her morning routine because otherwise she would have been here before me. She probably lives one or two blocks maximum east of me. Something had started to stir in the uncanny quiet and not before long it had evolved into a wall of cries. The ladies cried out requests for best friendship and the gentlemen had understood what I already had. Everyone in my box rammed against the gate and created a type of moshpit. I kept my calm in order to follow the development. My inner picture of her got updated by the second. You see, this is how us dogs get to know each other, by smelling each other's bums. And we don't have to put our nose to it. Do I desire to make acquaintances with her? Yes. I can't do more than join the line of admirers that this Dog Cave has become. But what I can do is to play this well and convince her to run away with me. The classic drama of Lady and the Tramp is for us what Romeo and Juliet is for humans. The impossible love is what we have learned to live with. We exchanged companionship among ourselves for security and food. Deformations were never part of the deal but that is a different story. We don't mind our new lives, we have grown accustomed but we will never forget where we come from. The distant howling from wolves tells of a life of constant insecurity. The brutal and unfair hunt has turned the wolves into living fossils much like the pandas. They are feared ghosts who are not accepted into a proposed time-share scheme as they are forced off the land with nowhere to go.

I left the frenzy that six small dogs had managed to create to position myself on the closest sofa. This gave me a fairly good view over the spectacle that was unfolding. I didn't see the entire place, only a fraction but from here I could keep surveillance using my fine senses, as there was too much chaos on the floor. Now followed a wave of silence and it approached our room. All the dogs by the gate shut up and looked to the right, they followed the object passing our cell by turning their head left. Soon she passed our gate; an Afghan Hound.

It all collapsed there and then, our eyes did meet and there was mutual affection, no doubt, but the problem portrayed in Lady and the Tramp was of another sort. This was not about class; it was the imposed racism that made our love impossible. I, an English toy terrier, will never be allowed to be near an afghan hound. I knew exactly how to gain her interest and I had pretty much already sealed the deal. She immediately grew bored of the unanimous group of admirers and her seeing me relaxed on the sofa was the only thing I needed to win her heart. But all in vain, we both knew the outcome and to expose our delicate hearts to the pain of being so close, yet so far apart, would render our lives terrible.

HARD COURT

PHOTOGRAPHY: JOHAN NILSSON
TEXT: ERIK NORDLANDER

A cycle from town. Eighty percent of success is showing up. The tennis court at Lilla Skuggan in Norra Djurgården. This place is so remote no pros come here, no talents. It is for the bon vivants, the flaneurs, where a straight one hand backhand is counted no higher than the heron flying by.

Where are we? Open fields, oak forest, dappled light, villas with royal ancestry, the sea. This is the setting. The opponent arrives, a member dressed with simplicity. The game starts. His serve breaks the silence in two, crows fly. An ace. How can he be that good? A champion. Someone who should be on the circuit. Who said tennis begins with love?

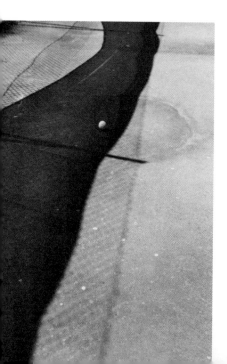

STOCKHOLMS SKÄRGÅRDS TENNISKLUBB. MEMBERS ONLY. MAKE FRIENDS.
ADDRESS: LILLA SKUGGANS VÄG.

REROUTE

SERGELS TORG

(ESCAPING UTOPIA)

TEXT: **JACOB BOHLIN**
PHOTOGRAPHY: **TOVE FREIIJ**

Upon leaving Stockholm, one of the least likely places to miss is Sergels torg. It is also one of the least likely places to miss upon arrival. Surveying Sergels torg from one of the high buildings that surround it, it was obviously built to act and be perceived as the hub of Stockholm city. Being the address of the main entrance to the central metro station, to some extent it is. Viewed from above, the great roundabout, centred around a 37 metre glass obelisk, that is surrounded by a fountain, dominates one's field of vision, truly giving the impression of a wheel spinning: a visual representation of a gear in that immense machinery in which we all are assumed to act as cogs.

At pedestrian level - the distinct, triangular-shaped chequered square, known as Plattan, meaning 'the Slab' - one finds that most Stockholmers try their best to avoid it, they hurry, they make for the shortest possible way out. When you find yourself here, do not panic. Neither follow the example of fleeing Stockholmers. Not yet, anyway. Instead, take your time to take this place, and the people who actually do spend time here, in. Most likely, you came here by metro. Note the throngs of people just outside the turnstiles, eager to greet whoever they are waiting for, soon to be on their way. Note the unusual number of loitering scene kids. Note the constant but shifting group of shady-looking types lurking around outside the entrance of Burger King. Note the nonchalantly parked police van.

There might be some kind of rally or demonstration going on. Events like that are common at the Slab, perhaps because the police – issuing the permits – appreciate how here, protesters are somewhat out of the way but still can't complain that they're being made invisible, standing as they do in the very centre of the capital.

Step outside, onto the Slab and have a look around. Squint your eyes and remember: this is Utopia. This is what the future used to look like, when it was still in its prime. This is the dream of modern man manifest. Towering in front of you, most likely blocking out the sun, should there be any, is Kulturhuset: theatres, libraries and exhibition spaces. Not bad, really.

On your right is a wide flight of stairs leading up to street level, in summer

the punks, tourists, addicts and the general stray tend to congregate here. On your left, the square continues, stretching into the darkness underneath the roundabout. Just a few years ago, that space looked like a gate to the underworld: a littered grotto, dimly lit in a strange green tone, like a fish tank long neglected. Today it's somewhat better, painted white. Still, it's time for you to take off.

Keep to the left along the underground part of the square, passing Burger King. Unless you're looking for heroin, avoid the shadies. Take the escalator out of the darkness and up into the bustling pedestrian high street, Sergelgatan. This is just our escape route; the homogeneity of the businesses on Sergelgatan is unrivalled. Ahead, on your right hand side, is another slice of Utopia: Hötorgsskraporna, a complex of high-rises originally intended to be much more than just office space. Here, just like on Sergels torg, the city-planners were into multi-level construction.

Surrounding the high-rises, terraces were to function as an open-air mall and all-over meeting point, teeming with shoppers and connected by footbridges to yet other terraces on top of the buildings across Sergelgatan. Like the Slab (and the nearby Malmskillnadsgatan for that matter, a notorious centre of street prostitution) the multi-level city design indeed showed to provide meeting points. However, it turned out many of them were favoured most of all by the city's less desired elements, and in the seventies the terraces were permanently shut due to 'social problems'.

Today locked gates block the stairs, crowned by sharp spikes and barbed wire. Now, the footbridge crossing Sergelgatan leads nowhere but into the wall of a row of 21st century condominiums, constructed on top of what was once one of these dilapidated terraces.

Sergelgatan isn't very long. Soon you'll find yourself on Hötorget, 'the Hay market'. With the fading importance of such commodities as hay and straw, the merchandise here today is mostly flowers, fruit, vegetables and the odd Bob Marley t-shirt. You may note how every greengrocer on the square carries the exact same product range. You will note how they all use the same cries, only so slightly shifting with the seasons: "Halva pris sparris!" (Spring), "Halva pris jordgubbar!" (Summer), "Halva pris kantareller!" (Autumn).

Contrarily to the Slab, Hötorget doesn't seem to be avoided at all. On sunny days people of all ages, means and walks of life frequent the stairs of Konserthuset, the Concert hall: smoking cigarettes, having lunch, drinking coffee. Coffee is easily obtained from Pressbyrån, 7-Eleven or one of the more fancy coffee shops in the Hötorgshallen market halls or the department store PUB. All are very close by. Hot dogs are bought at the kiosk by the fountain, strawberries

from the stalls, kebabs and merguez from the delis in Hötorgshallen. And conveniently, out of a box by the underground station: free Metro newspapers to sit on for those worried about pigeon droppings.

The building housing both Hötorgshallen and the multiplex cinematic theatre Filmstaden Sergel stands out as a seemingly successful example of architecture in the area. At night it's pretty to look at, with giant mosaics of broken-up meandering patterns brightly shining through the glass façade. During the day it's good to spy to out of, overlooking the market square from an elevated aspect.

In the basement, and part of the ground floor, is Hötorgshallen. Compared to market halls in many other European capitals it's really not that impressive, but it's probably the one place in Stockholm where you can get a rare Bordeaux, a bunch of fresh tomatillos and suckling pig all under one roof. Originally opened in 1959, this building was part of the great utopian plan, but it wasn't until 1995, after multiple retro refitting operations, that it arrived at its current layout.

Move upstairs, to the cinema, where you can take your suckling pig with you. There are 14 screens, and only children's films are dubbed, keeping most films intelligible also to non-Swedish speakers. Did I mention that this place is functionalistic too? Upon the ending of a show, some of the theatres even let you out through a different door, leading you into a backstreet – Slöjdgatan. The best way out is also the least obvious: squeezed between two newer buildings opposite the cinema's back exit, is a glassed-in passageway called Hötorgspassagen. Despite its red-glass sliding doors, and its retro-styled lit sign with a big arrow pointing you in their direction, this place is still easily missed, which is a shame as it houses one of the best coffee places in the city. There's never anywhere to sit at Caffetteria del Corso, but patrons stand around drinking coffee and talking, talking, talking. Once I counted at least eleven prime Italian gentlemen here.

Still savouring the round, chocolatey taste of espresso in your mouth, exit through the door towards Drottninggatan. Cast a quick eye to your left, spy the small portion of Kulturhuset showing a couple of blocks away to remind yourself of where you are, before you continue north, watching businesses grow less generic, the cityscape less utopian, and the people less heterogeneous with each step.

FIKA

TEXT: **ALISA GRIFO**
ILLUSTRATION: **THERESE VANDLING**

Let's meet for a fika? Do you have time for a fika today? What are you up to this afternoon, how about we grab a coffee? A bun? No bun? Ok, just a coffee or a chocolate biskvi or both? They work best together. A dammsugare? I know, you thought that means 'vacuum' in Swedish but it's also one of those little, green tube sweets you find at konditoris. You see them neatly lined up like soldiers in the case. Also to be found at Ikea in the deli section if you are not in Sweden any time soon. Don't forget the cocosbollar and the Princess cake, Prinsesstårta in Swedish. The ultimate fika treat. Made for a family with three princesses who were all very fond of the combination of marzipan, cream, sponge cake and sometimes raspberry jam. There is also a Prince cake to be fair to the boys but rarely will you find it in any respectable konditori.

What do we do during a fika? We talk, we huddle together, we speak in sombre tones or joyful silly voices if it's a good day. A day filled with sunshine and summer, devoid of melancholy and nostalgia. Children can come too, as you see, fika can feel like anything from a joyful children's party or a

94-year-old's wake. Tones and topics of joy and sadness abound.

Where to go? I can only make some suggestions in Stockholm, but every decent Swedish town has one form of a konditori or another, and if they don't they are likely to have a little cafe in the Coop (formally Konsum Grocery) or a 7-11. Fika is not required to be held at a konditori, although it certainly adds to the pleasure. So Stockholm it is, where most of the konditoris have aristocratic undertones in their mannerisms. Where one fills your own cup of coffee from the sideboard or centre table and in doing so you believe you are in 'Fanny and Alexander' for just one second of the afternoon. If you're with Grandma or you love cosy, grandmotherly places, go to **STUREKATTEN**. Filled with cosy chairs and frilly curtains, I recommend the room to the right at the top of the narrow, winding stairs. Take a table in the second room, all the way in the back, one with a small lamp on it. Conversation and sounds abound at Sturekatten, mostly hushed tones. You are in Östemalm, one of the more serious parts of town. Now that you have been to Grandma's head to

Grandpa's cafe, **VALAND**. If we were in Holland you would call this a brown cafe. It's woody and warm and still run by the original owner and his wife, the Åströms. Himself and the Valand interior he designed come from 1954. Good, strong Swedish coffee, not good sandwiches and decent sweets. Absolutely perfect if you are a recluse and in a reclusive mood, where you imagine yourself smoking a pipe in a 1950s den. Inspiring art on the walls and often empty. The neon above the kitchen made me realise the owner should be an artist and not pounding his feet around a cafe kitchen for 60 years. Extremely poetic place. If you are not keen on Grandma, Grandpa or the memories are too painful, I would suggest **RITORNO**, it has not failed me in 15 years. Outdoor seating in the summer; welcoming year round. Fantastic, traditional, Swedish sweets from the finest bulle to the most intricate Budapest cake with its peeled mandarin slices nestled in nut meringue. Pancakes too, the real ones that are slightly salty, that come with not the finest cream or jam, but they are made the way they "should be made". Strong, good coffee can be found at Ritorno, a requirement for any decent fika. **NYBERGS** in Odenplan has been slightly updated but still has a very comfortable cafe in the city feel. I consider their shrimp sandwich to be the best from the konditoris in Stockholm. **VETE-KATTEN** is a distant relative of Sturekatten. There is an older side with a curious 'Kajutan'

room near the ordering counter and a modern side as well. Oh, I should mention, at all konditoris ordering at the counter is de rigueur, as is self-service coffee, and refills are included. Coffee refills have their own words - påtår (one refill), tvåtår (second refill), tretår (third refill, that is pushing it!). Vete-Katten has so many rooms, seven at last count, plus an outdoor space, it is easy to get confused, bordering on lost. It took me ten years to realise they have a back area adjacent to the garden, head to the left of the kitchen to find it. And finally, the least traditional of my bunch, **CHIC KONDITORI** in Södermalm. Decent sweets and an assortment too. Not at all cosy, in fact down right East German in feel at best, but it does have its own special appeal, much like the TV tower of Stockholm, which harks back to the Cold War. Like every establishment in Stockholm its grime went the way of the new sanitary laws, however there remain traces of the mid-70s, if you ignore the new floor. They can get a little 'progressive' with their selection here, with odd flavours, and there are plenty of novelty sweets for the kids. They are the least traditional of the bunch. If you have no time for the first half of the 1900s head here.

What time to meet? Around 16:00. See you there. Let's talk.

STUREKATTEN
RIDDARGATAN 4
TEL: 08-611 1612

KONDITORI RITORNO
ODENGATAN 80-82
TEL: 08-32 01 06

VETE-KATTEN
KUNGSGATAN 55
TEL: 08-20 84 05

KONDITORI VALAND
SURBRUNNSGATAN 48
TEL: 08-30 04 76

NYBERGS
UPPLANDSGATAN 26
TEL: 08-32 11 95

CHIC KONDITORI
SWEDENBORGSGATAN 5A
TEL: 08-642 70 40

A CROOKED BACKSTREET AWAY

TEXT: **ALEXANDER HAVELDA**

PHOTOGRAPHY: **ERIK NORDLANDER**

The sun is only true object of worship to the atheist Swede, but if one were to describe Stockholm's divinity, sunny would not be it.

Stockholm's spiritual characteristic lies rather in its calmness.

Not the calmness of indifference, conceived in boredom or by giving up. No, the calmness of Stockholm is, much like the calmness of religion, rather characterised by the fact that it's never further than a crooked backstreet away from life's pleasures.

All of Stockholm's vices are surrounded by quiet, modest water, reluctantly dressed in gold, and most blocks lean against parks or forests. Some against mountains. In every busy street there is always something slow and no matter the fount of a suddenly risen pulse, the consolidation of silence and simple colours is always near.

If God is always watching and always available, calmness is Stockholm's God.

There are a million examples of the sudden divine calmness in Stockholm. Since I don't have the time or knowledge to tell you about them all, I would like to take you for a walk in my home area Södermalm, and tell you about a few of the watering holes I usually take refuge in, when I seized by a sudden urge for spiritual rest.

To truly demonstrate that Stockholm's calmness is available even in places full of life, our walk will take place around Södermalm's busiest shopping street, Götgatan. None of the places I will take you to are located further than a couple of hundred metres from this street.

Our walk starts at the Maria Magdalena graveyard, located a shout away from Götgatan. Despite this, the graveyard is quiet and calm, occupied only by a thousand fragile tulips. Like red-lipped teenagers, they don't give a fuck about time or place. They just sway peacefully under masculine oak trees and a church bell, tolling with gentle reproach every fifteen minutes.

Our cat, Katty Perry, used to play among the tulips during our first autumn in this block. Then she got locked in our neighbour's basement and starved to death. She was never buried. We got her back in a plastic bag by those who found her. I don't know what happened with the bag, but looking back, I feel we should have tried to bury her in the graveyard. We should have sneaked in there during the night and dug a hole next to Sweden's national poet, Evert Taube. There's plenty of room between his grave and the next one, belonging to the bus driver.

To find the next serenity spot, open the graveyard gate and enter Sankt Paulsgatan. Walk up the street and after you've passed a comic shop, an espresso bar and a tattoo parlour, you'll find yourself at the corner of Sankt Paulsgatan and Götgatan.

Here lies a fancy clothing store that is sadly out of place, trying to trade bourgeois clothing brands on an island where people's vanity is mainly manifested by alternative gestures. Despite his looks, the owner of the store is a lonely narcissist, longing for a person to share his aesthetic values. Besides the compulsory Robyn track, the shop is always calm end empty. Open the door. Say Hi! to him, as if you thought he were cute. He will let you sit there for hours. Maybe he will offer you a cup of coffee. If you're a girl, I'll bet you can even get him to turn the Robyn track off.

On the other side of Götgatan awaits a few other relaxing joints.

Take a right up Götgatan. Then take a left at Högbergsgatan and you'll pass a nice little shop selling bolts and door handles. The shop has been owned by the same family for almost a hundred years. The first time I passed by, I was impressed by how pretty it was, and curious to see how it looked inside. For some reason it took four years and fifty walks before I entered, or rather before I tried. The door handle was stuck, I never made it in. I have, however, heard that the voiceless owner lets visitors wait for their turn until they leave, and that his Thai mistress, who visits the shop during daylight, ashamed by his ignorance, offers pseudo-customers Maryland Cookies and rosé wine. If you have a few minutes to spare, you should enter for fika.

Further up Högbergsgatan you'll see a beautiful balcony filled with plants and mighty furniture, worthy of any syphilitic Victorian. Standing beneath it, you can still hear people skateboard or eat bacon on Götgatan. The owner of the balcony is the guy who came up with the Absolut vodka font. I don't know much about him, but I think that he's Norwegian and that he has an anorexic, eunuch housekeeper. Every now and then, a piece of furniture falls off his balcony, and it usually takes a long time before he picks it up. One time, as I was passing by, I noticed a stuffed crow lying on the ground. If you feel like sitting down for a smoke, I suggest you jump over the fence and have a look. You might find yourself a damaged Chesterfield and some cigarette butts.

Walk twenty metres more, until the end of Högbergsgatan, and you have reached our walk's final destination, the Katarina graveyard.

Go in.

The graveyard resembles an old person's living room, dropped down

in-between outdated facades, neatly
decorated with rabbits, in-between
a soft, green carpet and mortality
dangling in the air.

It has always been my favourite
spot in Södermalm. Before I read on
Wikipedia that the corpses from the
biggest massacre in Swedish history,
The Bloodbath of Stockholm, were
burnt there, before I saw the Katarina
church burn on TV in 1990, before
I found out that Swedish foreign
minister Anna Lind, who was stabbed
by a guy in a 'Just Do It' cap, is buried
in the middle of the lawn, I liked it here.

I suggest you stand under one of
the graveyard trees. Wait until a bird
cries and the walls around answer.
Soon, leaves or snow will fall from
the wooden fingers above your head.
These are the fingers of Stockholm's
God. When you are bored, do not
despair - life's pleasures are only a
crooked backstreet away.

LEARNING TO GROW

A WALK THROUGH BERGIANSKA TRÄDGÅRDEN

KRISTIN LARSSON, SIMON SKUTELI & ERIK NORDLANDER

Bergianska Trädgården is a botanical garden forgotten by many, but by no means neglected.

If you are at the central part of town around T-centralen, or Östermalmstorg, take the red metro line towards Mörby centrum. Get off at Universitetet and walk left, past the Museum of natural history. You may stop here if you want to see the skeleton of a Tyrannosaurus Rex or Blue Whale. Mind you, there are good things waiting ahead.

Once you have walked past the museum you will face a small hill with oaks and bright, yellow houses. If you happen to be here in May, stop and gaze at all the apple trees in full bloom. Take a left, cross the railway and enter the botanical garden.

Since this is a botanical garden it is a place for acquiring knowledge and not just for strolling. There is a great diversity of plants and some parts such, as the large greenhouse, are like a living museum. There are parts where plants grow in 'free' landscapes, wetlands where spontaneous materials are brought in from the surrounding nature, as well as segments with plants from North America and Asia.

Most specific to the garden are the amount of crop plants. The Bergius brothers, who founded the garden, were focused on teaching gardeners, and by extension the Swedish people, how to cultivate crops with the motto that the Swedish people should be able to be self-sufficient. The Bergianska Trädgården has more orchards, vegetables and berries than other botanical gardens in Sweden.

The café Gamla Orangeriet (The Old Orangery) is lovely for cake, coffee or a glass of wine. Victoriahuset, a beautiful greenhouse shaped like a dome, is also quite special, inhabited by tropical giant water lilies (the greatest water lilies in the world, actually) since the beginning of the 20th century. The name of this plant house has nothing to do with the Swedish crown princess Victoria Bernadotte, whose residence can be spotted just across the water, but derives from the giant water lilies of the Victoria family. It's open to visitors for a small fee, from beginning of May to late September.

The vantage point at the back of the garden, enclosed by white balustrades, offers a view of Brunnsviken, the body of water below. Here, people sunbathe

in the summer, and during the winter skate or cross country ski across the ice. There's a large, pine tree in the middle of the vantage point and benches to rest upon. The pine tree is old, and there is a sign that will tell you to stay away if the wind is too strong.

One of the gardeners is called Kaili. She is responsible for everything that is edible in the garden. She is from Estonia and we ask her about how she ended up here. She tells us she studied gardening in Estonia and that her family was crazy for plants. Later she also worked as a farmer. She moved to Sweden to find a new life, and of course she wanted to visit a botanical garden. She remembers her first visit to Bergianska: a bright light through the spruce hedge, the light in the orangery and the water lilies in the Victoriahuset, which she says, "seemed a little mysterious". She joined a class for immigrants to learn Swedish, and when given the task to interview a Swedish person, decided to return and interview the gardener at the Bergianska Trädgården. Two years later she herself became a gardener here.

Continue your route, guided by the flowers, grasses, bushes and trees, learn from nature, learn how to grow.

BENNINGE LAND

EVERY MAN'S RIGHT TO ROAM

TEXT: **OSCAR CARLSON**
PHOTOGRAPH: **MARTIN BENNINGE**

Countries spend much effort disputing borders and laying claim to lands. This is an exercise thought to be exclusive to countries but one summer day, Stockholm socialite Martin Benninge felt he had discovered a spot so full of wonder, he named it Benninge Land.

Between two trees at the far end of some kind of boot camp sports ground, there is a path. The path will take you through the closest thing you get to a jungle in Sweden. Walking over rocks, through blueberry shrubs, pushing cobwebbed pine tree branches away from your face, you will be rewarded with nothing short of a scene depicted in beer commercials trying to convey the perfect summer. Here you will find small wind-battered trees and round granite cliffs that provide excellent platforms to dive off into the cool waters.

The view of the water, with sailboats passing in front of a large number of little islands, is very pleasing. After a reasonable bus ride and walk, you will find yourself relatively close to the city, yet with no buildings in sight.

Martin explains that he and his friends thought it was amazing that you could access the archipelago without having to take a boat.

The story goes that the first time Martin went there was with a girlfriend. Her best friend had told her about some cliffs, prefect for swimming off, that only the locals knew about. This recommendation came from the best friend's boyfriend that had a summer residence located nearby.

Martin dumped his girlfriend but kept returning, and soon Martin started calling it his island. Martin actually admits that it was Betty that started calling it Benninge Land. Betty confirms this: "All I know is that the first time I met anyone from this group it was there. Martin invited Julie and I to join. I want to say we came up with it since he kept calling it his island. But later we found out that Lisa had discovered it as a child."

Exercising every man's right to roam - allemansrätten, and the implemented protection of beaches - strandskyddet, means everyone can and should enjoy the archipelago in the summer. This gem is welcome to all, but you should expect a group of fifteen friends, acting as if they owned the place, waving a little, white flag saying: Benninge Land.

HOW TO GET THERE:
TAKE BUS 428X FROM SLUSSEN AND GET OFF AT STORA SAND.
COORDINATES: 59.213318, 18.515066

VAXHOLM

REVISITING A DAD JOKE

TEXT: **OSCAR CARLSON**
PHOTOGRAPH: **MÄRTA THISNER**

Pretty much every Dad has a number of jokes, or if you are unlucky just one, that he insists on telling over and over again. You grow up hearing your dad's terrible jokes and will most likely end up terrorizing your own kids with them, who in turn will make sure this oral tradition is performed by many generations to come.

In Sweden, Dad jokes stand in contrast to the ordinary jokes that often make fun of neighbouring countrymen, are plain racist or come out of the subconscious protestant anxiety. Dad jokes, however, are usually slapstick and delivered deadpan with a sexist twist.

There is one joke that I thought only my Dad has in his thin, but not lacking substance, repertoire, until someone else said that their Dad also had been rolling the same joke. The joke turned out to be widely spread and it goes like this: The German field commander, Helmuth von Moltke, laughed twice in his life, once when his mother-in-law died and the other time when he paid a visit to the fortress of Vaxholm.

Von Moltke the elder was Chief of Staff, renowned and rewarded for modernising the Prussian army in the mid-nineteenth century. The construction of the fortress in Vaxholm was completed in 1863, after thirty years of construction, by which time the design had become hopelessly out of fashion. A test shooting showed that the walls would not stand the firepower of modern weaponry and so, instead, it became administrative headquarters.

The joke still flourishes and is perhaps a way for Sweden's men to deal with the loss of the military superpower they once held. Despite all this, the fortress is worth a visit. Beautifully located on the water outside the quaint harbour town, Vaxholm, officially a city on sixty-four islands. The fortress is now a museum, it not only puts mannequins with seventies haircuts on display, it also offers pleasant food and accommodation.

WWW.VAXHOLMSFASTNING.SE
WWW.STROMMA.SE/SV/KASTELLET-VAXHOLM

THE PHALLUS OF STOCKHOLM

TEXT: **KATARINA BOHLIN**
PHOTOGRAPH: **JOHAN NILSSON**

To spend a day looking down onto and beyond the city. Feeling small, tall and free, disconnected like nothing really matters. Being the king of the world. My expectations of Kaknästornet were pretty high, maybe too high for a 155-metre building from the sixties?

Didn't help either that the preparations, which might have provided some resistance, just rolled out like a red carpet. The bus 69K says Kaknästornet with large, shining letters and well, it takes you there, right there. It's a nice ride too, it rolls along the water and then onto the outskirts of the large, green area known as Gärdet.

I'd done my homework and the most memorable parts had stuck:

The tower was built to a tight time schedule, so tight that the architects Hans Borgström and Bengt Lindroos were still drawing as it was being constructed.

The windows of the restaurant and the two view-point floors are coated with a thin layer of gold, to keep some of the warmth from the sun out.

The elevator ride up to the 30th floor takes 30 seconds.

Standing on terra firme looking up, the tower looks like a star.

It has to do with squares and 45 degree angles, but the end result is a star. I walked in on bubbly-light feet. The tired guy in the combined entrance/souvenir shop took my 50 kronor bill and let me in; I chose the left elevator and had my watch ready as I pressed the button.

It really did take 30 seconds as I followed the 30 red lights inside the elevator light up and then go dark again as I rose higher. On the 30th second, we stopped and the doors opened.

I was facing a long table covered with sandwiches, cookies and cakes, with bright red and green jello toppings. A bit confused, I stuck my head out, two men were having a telephone conference at a table by one of the large windows, to my right and a young girl and her mother were having fika.

From one side of the tower you see the city below, and from the opposite side you can see observe how the archipelago is formed, with ferries and tankers sailing in and out. You can see as far as sixty kilometres on a clear day. It was clear, I think I did.

I took the stairs up to the top view-point, which just has a fence around and above it and signs telling you not to throw stuff out over the edge as someone below might get hurt. I took two laps around the tower, wind in my hair, thinking about what I read downstairs outside the elevators, that the highest floors can swing up to 30 centimetres from side to side on a windy day. It was, and I think it did.

Right then, looking down on the teeny-tiny people walking around on the grass, doll house-sized horses in a pen and my apartment building far away to my right, in a grey tower, high above a city about to go into summer slumber, it happened.

THE CITY IS A BATTLEFIELD

TEXT: **KATARINA BOHLIN**

PHOTOGRAPHY: **BEATRICE FERNQVIST**

Don't let anyone fool you, don't kid yourself. There are minefields, borders and no man's land, areas where camouflage is necessary and places you shouldn't enter without kevlar.

During the last five months I've dated and then not dated three men, all of them living in or hanging around the neighbourhood of Vasastan. So from Odenplan, the heart of Vasastan, where I generally get off the tunnelbana (underground), to S:t Eriksplan where my work is so conveniently located, I've created a route with places to disappear.

Things are under control, there are no attacks or counter attacks but I'm trying to avoid unexpected encounters with Someone on a bad hair day or the worst, sidewalk meetings with Someone walking along with a potential new someone-else. Those meetings need hours of styling, grooming and general armouring.

Most likely, you won't find yourself in a war of hearts during your stay. However, my collection of hideouts can give you shelter on a rainy day, or simply when you want some peace and quiet.

The fastest way to get to S:t Eriksplan from Odenplan is via Odengatan, which is also the busiest street and therefore means more people and higher risk. Don't be a chicken, choose Odengatan.

If like me, you have arrived there on the underground, you will get off at Karlbergsvägen. Odengatan is the street parallel to Karlbergsvägen, with Odenplan in between. Cross the square to get to Odengatan.

The small antique shop called **EPOK** at 83, Odengatan is the first stop. It's perfect since it is small and dark, and you'll want to stay there for a long time, admiring all the jewellery, wristwatches and hats. I've been there three times on missions to find and buy, but the owner's been consequently unwilling to sell me anything, so don't feel obliged to spend money whilst hiding.

As you walk down Odengatan, you will pass by Gustav Vasa church and there you'll find some pleasant restaurants with outdoor seating, such as **PRIMO CIAO CIAO** on Odengatan and **TENNSTOPET** on the corner of Odengatan and Dalagatan. Have an espresso or a meal if you like, but bear in mind, you're an easy target on a chair on the pavement...

Going further down Odengatan is Vasaparken to your left, this is a lovely, big park with a football/ice hockey field and large green areas. Stay away, lots of people means danger.

Sneak in at **KONDITORI RITORNO** at 80, Odengatan. The outdoor seating is popular, but the inside is large and cool in the summer, and almost empty. They serve sandwich cake, a classical Swedish dish common at christenings and communions.

If you're ambushed, retreat to philosophical conversation at **FORUM** at 14, Sigtunagatan or to the hair salon at 7, Hälsingegatan. This place is like the interior of an old lady's living room, complete with plaid blankets, ruched pillows and silk lampshades. Inhale the soothing scent of lilacs and regroup.

Flee down the last part of Odengatan, after you've passed the lower end of Vasaparken you'll find yourself at a small, open spot with two underground exits on each side of a street. Cross the street to S:t Eriksgatan and you've arrived. Celebrate staying alive and unharmed for another day with a **TOSCA** nut piece at **MELLQVIST** at 4, Rörstrandsgatan, or a cardamom roll at **BRÖD&SALT** at 15, Birkagatan, where the plans for new battles on undiscovered turf may take shape.

A PLACE OF REST

TEXT & PHOTOGRAPHY: **BILLIE LINDAHL**

To get to Skogskyrkogården (the cemetery in the forest) the easiest way, take the green subway line heading south. The station is named after the cemetery, so you can't go wrong. When you emerge you will see a suburban street and a stone wall, walk along until you enter the cemetery, you will find yourself miles away from traffic. In front of you is a field with gentle, rolling hills to the right, and to the left you can see a granite cross, cutting into the sky. Further away is the forest.

This cemetery is built around grass and trees. You can smell the pine needles in the air, but this is not a wild place. It has been carefully designed and planned. If you follow the stone steps up to the hill, you will notice the steps gets smaller and smaller the further up you go. It is made that way so that the visitor won't tire whilst climbing. And then, if you leave the circle of trees and walk down the other side, you will reach a wide pathway that runs straight through the woods. Birches grow on the side, but after a while the forest changes to pine, and when you reach the end of the pathway, large firs close in on you. It is

made that way, to allow for mourners to feel their grief as they walk towards the funeral chapel. The chapel of resurrection is usually closed but if it is open, go inside. It has only one window but you will still perceive it as bright. The walls and floors are white, and the flow of light is only interrupted by the rows of black chairs. There are two more chapels to look at, but perhaps you should just take a walk among the stones in the woods. To hurry is not the point here. Walk slowly, look at the names, look at the flowers. If you have company you will have plenty of space to talk about all sorts of things, little and big. And if you feel like having a day to yourself, this is the ultimate place to go. You won't feel lonely, there are many people around. After all this place is made both for the dead and the living.

RISING UP

TEXT & PHOTOGRAPHY: **ERIK NORDLANDER**

You meet up, you sign a paper, you get into a small bus. You drive to a field where the bus driver turns out to be your captain. He releases a small, red balloon in order to check the wind direction. He follows it with his large, old-school binoculars.

The idea is that you take off from the side of town according to the direction of the wind. Like that you travel across and land somewhere on the other side.

Our captain is not pleased with the direction of the balloon and we are ordered to get back onto the bus. Our co-passengers, a group of Israelis working for Ericsson, make fun of each other. One of them is squashed against the radiator of the bus, the captain's assistant, seated at the front of the bus, is trying to switch it off. The assistant is sweating and the Israeli guy's leg fries against the radiator, his comrades laugh and shout that their friend's leg will soon be 'well done'.

Finally, we alight in a grass field in Nacka, where we begin to unfold the balloon and generate the fans that will fill it with air. The balloon is huge.

The basket is not very large, there are certainly larger ones, and it fits 12 people, it is divided into six compartments. As we are about to rise, the temperature from the aggregate is higher than in a sauna. Remember to bring a cap! Then we rise, and the silence is total between the hot flames jetting above the captain's wrist.

Suddenly we are over the water - 300, and then 400 metres above the sea. Stockholm is to the left and the archipelago to the right. We sail towards Lidingö, and the Israelis bring out candy and seem amused. As we glide down, they take pictures of impressive villas.

We sail even lower. People in apartment buildings are keen to wave at us, whole families emerge onto their balconies. The people in the large villas, on the other hand, are little intrigued. A social experiment better than most.

We land without trouble in a field in Djursholm. It is hard work to fold the balloon but the Israelis work hard. I wonder how six old ladies would have managed? I think about what the farmer will say when he finds out. Undoubtedly we have caused some damage. Perhaps fines are absorbed into in the fee we have paid.

We are baptised as counts, barons and duchesses of Djursholm, and we return home, a nice adventure complete, the perspective suitably changed.

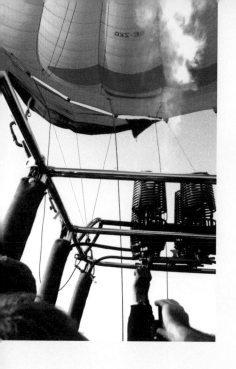

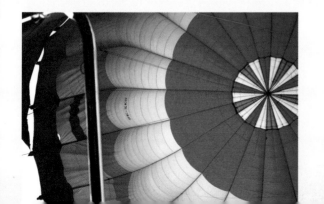

ITINERARY: KUNGSHOLMEN

TEXT: **ANNE LAURELLA**
PHOTOGRAPHY: **PAUL QUANT**

AN ISLAND IN THE CITY

Kungsholmen is the best part of the inner city to live in, and the least obvious to visit. Of those elements usually spotted on a brisk visit to a city - museums, art galleries, restaurants and clubs, there are plenty more of these in other neighbourhoods of Stockholm. Historically, Kungsholmen has been a place for monks, artisans, prostitutes, working class folk and industry. It is only in modern times, during the last ten years, that the image of the dreary, relatively uneventful neighbourhood is being erased.

Let me explain:

THE LONG WALK

Walking around Kungsholmen is probably the best way to get to know a large part of the western part of Stockholm. The promenade running along the waterfront is about 10 kilometres long and here, you will pass through a variety of settings - you'll discover not only the island you are on, but also all those that surround it. Put on comfortable shoes - and if it's hot outside - bring your swimsuit! Of course you can begin your walk wherever you want, but we suggest Stockholms stadshus (the Stockholm City Hall), at Norr Mälarstrand, as the start. The footpath from the city hall to Rålambshovsparken is as busy as an autobahn during holiday time - it's here the Kungsholmen residents find time to stroll, jog, walk the dog, walk the kids, sit by the water or enjoy a drink at one of the bars. And rightly so as Stockholm, though surrounded by water, does not offer other promenades such as this. Our walk starts with the view of half the city - from Riddarholmen, Södermalm and Långholmen to the massive bridge Västerbron, which threads Södermalm and Kungsholmen together.

Norrmälarstrand holds some tragic and morbid events. In 1932 at No.24, there happened what would become one of the most high-profile cases in Swedish criminal history - the von Sydowska murders. The circuit judge and politician Hjalmar von Sydow, together with two of his domestics were found slain. When the main suspect, the drug addicted son Fredrik von Sydow, was called in for questioning he went ahead of the entire justice system by shooting his wife Ingun, and then himself.

A more modern drama, that almost got as much media attention, was the so-called Tree Murder in 2011. Six of the large willows that line the walkway was sabotaged by someone who drilled holes in the stems and injected poison. This took place in front of No. 8 and it is said to have been done by someone who simply wanted a better view of the water.

As the air is filled with smoke from disposable barbecues and spilled beer, you know that you are soon approaching Rålambshovsparken, 'Rålis'. Here suburban kid gangs jostle with the residents of Kungsholmen for barbecues and boule tournaments. Walk towards Smedsuddsvägen, a child-friendly sandy beach and continue the walk taking a more adventurous direction. What was previously an accessible walking trail now submerges under Essingeleden, in the form of a forest trail that winds over the rocks along the water, away towards Fredhällsbadet.

Underneath the bridge Essingebron, Kungsholmen greets one of its siblings, Lilla Essingen. Lilla (little) and Stora (Great) Essingen was once 'the place' where the rich industrialists built their summer houses, though this part nowadays belong to central Stockholm.

Did you resist the urge to swim at Smedsuddsbadet? It is perhaps more difficult when you get to Fredshällsbadet, one of Stockholm's first sunbathing and swimming spots, which opened in the early 20th century. Now you have done about a third of the stretch, so have fika up at Solstugan (only during the summer months) and continue walking towards Kristinebergs strand, and the island's newest neighbourhood Hornsbergs strand. This neighbourhood has popped up over the past year and its promenade is one of the most successful projects within modern architecture in Stockholm. Here you will find a natural meeting place for the new, predominantly young residents. Restaurants and bars have opened along the quays of which restaurant Piren has quickly acquired a good reputation. You can also barbeque, have your own picnic, or just sit and read or watch the people passing by.

The last third of the walk around Kungsholmen runs along the canal Karlbergs kanal with the castle Karlbergs slott on one side and picturesque allotments of private plantations on the other. Watch the boats slowly chug up in the canal, and the plants. If it is afternoon or evening, have a late lunch or dinner at Flippin' Burgers. It is known as the city's best burger joint, which the cue outside testifies to. The circle is closed when you once again arrive at city hall and face the stream of tourists. You can be pleased knowing that you've seen a genuine part of Stockholm that many will miss.

A SHORTER WALK

If you rather prefer going straight for the heart of the island, choose Hantverkargatan which is one of the oldest streets in Kungsholmen, and cuts through the western half of the island, from the city hall up to Fridhemsplan. The street got its name in the 17th century, when artisans where lured with the promise of ten-year tax exemption. Among the guilds who moved here were tanners, glaziers, stocking knitters, hat makers and minters. The street was also lined by hospitals. At Eira kurhus, 'No. 13', prostitutes were cured for their STDs, yielding Kungsholmen a miserable reputation. The address today hosts Ekobrottsmyndigheten (the Authority for Economic Crimes), but the actual street number 13 is removed. Too big a shame, perhaps, for the state officials...

Arrive at the church Kungsholms kyrka and turn right at Kaplansbacken. At the top of the hill you will find a block called Kungsklippan. Here five, white functionalist high-rises scout over the city and the area is among the best examples of the changes that took place in Stockholm around the early 20th century. Previously the mountain was home to miserable and dilapidated shacks housing the poor.

When returning to Hantverkargatan via Parmmätargatan take the opportunity to travel down to Bergsgatan that, like a surging wave, moves from Kaplansbacken to Kronoberget. On Bergsgatan the district court, police station and jail sit side by side. There is also an excellent delicatessen which is hidden in a garage, at number 24. It is called Wijnjas grossisthandel and here they sell French and Italian cheeses of all kinds; it is a Stockholmer pilgrimage to stock up for the pleasures of the weekend. Further down, where Bergsgatan crosses Scheelegatan you will find Engströms Trikåaffär a small lingerie shop from the 19th century. In there time has stood still; you order over the counter and the saleswoman picks the articles out of hundred-year-old wooden boxes.

Back at Hantverkargatan continue across the street and choose the parallel street Garvargatan. This dark and narrow street was once part of the industrial, thumping heart of Kungsholmen. The old brick factories are still there - now apartments and offices - fortunately, gone is the stench of tanned animal hides. Follow Garvargatan westward and the atmosphere changes considerably as the square Kungsholmstorg opens up in all its majestic 19th century splendour.

Continue along Hantverkargatan, upwards towards Kartagos backe, where horse cabs once struggled uphill - until you reach the beautiful brick fire station on the right. If you follow Kronobergsgatan you soon hit Kronobergsparken, an oasis of Kungsholmen where the local children, sunbathers and drunkards share the green grass under the chestnut trees. In one corner of the park is a small Jewish cemetery, which may seem odd, but as with much else here is explained by history. In the 1780s this hill was still so remote that the members of the

Mosaic congregation thought it would be ideal to build a cemetery here, far away from the city noise.

From 'quiet Kronis' follow Drottningholmsvägen down to the more hectic Fridhemsplan. A little over ten years ago, Fridhemsplan was no more than a transport hub for commuters travelling westward. It is an important hub for subway and bus lines. Fridhemsplan has grown, and now has a shopping mall, several large supermarkets and many small shops. There are Italian ice cream parlours, Arabic tobacco dealers selling fruit tobacco for shisha, Asian grocery stores, a Hare Krishna centre and salsa clubs. Take the opportunity to stroll around on Fridhemsplan. There are plans to restore and rebuild, and then this part might become homogenous and bland.

COFFEE, LUNCH, DRINKS, DINNER, PARTY

For coffee and light lunches there are several gems to choose from: **BULLEBODEN** at Parmätargatan 7 bakes its own bread and serves hearty salads for lunch. In summer you can sit outside and admire Kungsholms kyrka.

IL CAFFÉ, at Bergsgatan 17, offers good Italian coffee and grilled sandwiches, a cool bar hangout providing a quiet moment under the trees next to the Rådhuset.

At **POLI CAFÉ**, S:t Göransgatan 70, you take a caffé Italiano, on the go, and you can talk to the regulars who come here.

One of Stockholm's most charming coffee bars is **ESPRESSOBAREN SORELLE**, Fridhemsgatan 15 – to the tones of Reggae, enjoy good coffee, sandwiches and fresh salads.

For a more wholesome lunch or dinner go to classic restaurant **MÄSTER ANDERS**, at the junction between Pipersgatan/Hantverkargatan, here they serve a mix of traditional Swedish food and French bistro.

Almost at the top of Hantverkargatan, number 81, you will find **WESTERMALMS SUSHI** – great sushi with Scandinavian inspiration and consideration for the environment, with tuna and giant shrimp removed from the menu.

RESTAURANG AG, tucked away among car service depots at Kronobergsgatan 37, has become known for its meat, **MÄLARPAVILJONGEN** on Norrmälarstrand 64 for its atmosphere and **LUX** at Lilla Essinge for their Michelin stars.

For a drink or two **ORANGERIET** at Norrmälarstrand is recommended, likewise **BOULEBAR** in Rålambshovsparken is good for activity seekers. Later at night party people moves towards **LOKAL** or perhaps, for those who really love Eurovision-pop, **LEMONBAR**. It must be expected to leave the island if you want to dance the night away. Heading back to Kungsholmen in the wee hours, you will notice one thing - the light. Light, bright purple and pale blue and then almost mint green. It is so beautiful in early summer, a joyful Stockholm melancholy.

ITINERARY: SÖDERMALM

TEXT: **TOVE ERIKSEN HILLBLOM**
ILLUSTRATION: **REBECKA BEBBEN ANDERSSON**
PHOTOGRAPHY: **GUSTAV ELLIOT**

Södermalm, never referred to as anything but Söder by locals, is perhaps the most diverse part of the city.

Traditionally the home of the working class, the drunks and the struggling artist/musician, Söder has over the past couple of decades become home to the not-so-struggling artist/musician/designer/coffee shop owner, while still keeping a touch of its rough past.

A new versus old mixture of people, it is also a true mixture of scenery; in no other part of the city will you find the same blend of quirky shops, kayakers, dodgy bars, tapas hideaways, beaches, vintage shops and spectacular views, catering for any mood swing its inhabitants may have.

Perhaps unsurprisingly then, as the working week draws to a close, Söder quickly swells with people leisurely roaming the island, in search of anything from a beer on a bobbing jetty, to the perfect pair of shoes.

On a summer morning, walk from Kungsholmen to the west part of Söder called Hornstull, crossing the majestic concrete and iron arc that is Västerbron.

Built in 1935, it finally allowed Hornstull residents to get to the city centre without having to take the boat.

When standing at the top of the bridge, it is as if the bridge itself is the divider between man and nature; looking east at the rising sun bathing the city in morning light, you see the density of a city comprised of 17th century buildings, office blocks, subway trains, theatres and squares, irregularly punctuated by church towers, like needles on a giant pin board.

Looking west, there is only water and lush green trees, with the odd building scattered around, crumbs fallen from the city cake. The feeling is that if like in the famous song you would chose to go west, you could go on forever.

Stroll slowly until you get to Hornstull, and make a right. 50 metres down the road you will find **LASSE I PARKEN**, a café and restaurant situated in a small, red cottage surrounded by a cosy, little garden. There has been some sort of restaurant or bar activity here since the middle of the 18th century and the old house is tiny, so watch your head as you step inside onto the well-worn, slightly skewed wooden floor.

In the evenings, as coffee is traded in for beers, little coloured lights speckle the night sky, and the garden fills up with live music.

Continue down the road and walk across the small bridge connecting Hornstull with Långholmen, a tiny island that used to be the prison island of Stockholm. Now the island is associated with far more leisurely activities and works as a quick visit to the countryside for those who still want to remain in the middle of the city. Make your way around the island on the narrow gravel walkway and hide from the world for a minute or two in one of the small, lilac-scented glades.

As you continue, you will discover a village-like miniature community of garden allotments, originally created in 1835 for the prison workers to be able to grow their own vegetables.

Nowadays, the allotments are extremely sought-after by city residents of all ages and the waiting list is estimated to be well over ten years (the last time an allotment was made available was four years ago).

On hot days, as the path opens up to a slanting park ending in a grand, sandy beach (by Swedish city standards), the soundtrack quickly changes - from the sound of your own footsteps accompanied by the odd bird, to that of shrieking seagulls and excited screams from people daring to swim in the cold water. As clothes are torn off, the choice of tattoos becomes the main means of identifying the mix of people that have come here; Batman-covered shoulders, calves cheering on a football team or arms acting as the canvases of artsy drawings and graphic patterns; this is a place most people can subscribe to.

At the other end of the park is **STORA HENRIKSVIK**, a wooden villa, painted in yellow, where you can treat yourself to hearty, home-made food, serving baked cakes, buns and more. Most of it is ecological, and as much as possible is made from what is grown in the 18th century garden. Although busy in the weekends and on holidays, the atmosphere is always one of relaxation.

Although one can quite happily spend an entire day here watching the sun travel across the sky, getting coffee refills - and you can even stay over in the hotel located in the converted prison building - a more urban experience is not far away should one crave it.

After leaving Långholmen, walk alongside the kayakers, past the pizza place with the far-too-cheap lager that draws a dubious crowd, and head towards Hornstulls strand where you will find something for every time of day. Here, you can count on the ratio between Batman vs. artsy tattoos to dramatically swing over towards the latter.

If you fancy a movie but aren't keen on the latest Tom Cruise blockbuster, slip in to **BIO RIO** (Hornstulls strand 3), one of Stockholm's few independent cinemas. You'll not only be treated to some lovely, well-preserved 1940s décor, you'll also be able to choose from a great selection of films, and, tada! Live opera! Spend

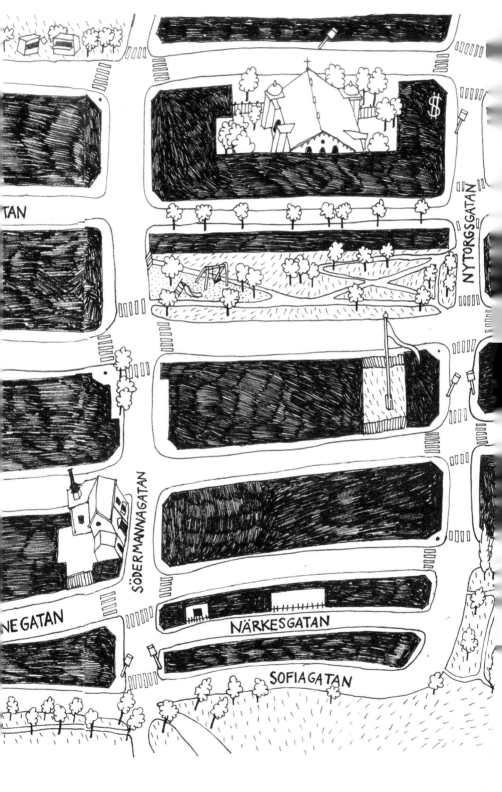

your Sunday morning here, enjoying one of their breakfast screenings, always specially themed (and yes, you are allowed to eat whilst watching).

Next door you'll find the vegan **COPACABANA CAFÉ**. The coffee is normally a little too hot but the seats outside, overlooking the old factories across the water, make up for it.

Should you want to present your taste buds with a feast on a level well beyond coffee and sandwiches, try the Asian-inspired restaurant **BARBRO** (Hornstulls strand 13). The atmosphere is as casual as the food is delicious and its concept of middle-sized dishes allows for a thorough exploring of the menu. Make sure not to miss out on the beef sashimi, spicy tuna or the lamb with pumpkin purée. (Note: this concept also means there's no real definition of when you should stop ordering more, which can be hazardous). **BARBRO** also collaborates with **BIO RIO**; after dinner, take the stairs down to the basement where you can sit comfortably in a sofa or lounge chair and watch a movie, enjoying full service from the bar.

Even closer to the water, clad in random, colourful mosaic resembling an oversized bathroom décor of a theme park, you'll find **STRAND DEBASER HORNSTULL** that consists of the French restaurant **FRANSKA ÖPPNA**, **BAR BROOKLYN** and **DEBASER** itself, offering live gigs and a night club.

NIGHT-TIME DETOUR

Should you feel a tingling, romantic sensation after a couple of drinks and should you be lucky, the club night **NATTEN** might be on. To get there, you'll need to hike across Liljeholmsbron to Färgfabriken (Lövholmsbrinken 1), an old paint factory turned into a nightclub. Natten offers pure 100% slow dancing to the most romantic ballads in pop history, even the most cynical is guaranteed to fall for this unique atmosphere, where hundreds of people lay aside their cool for a moment and suddenly find themselves kissing a complete stranger under the magic, light summer sky. (Check out www.natten.eu for dates - if there's nothing coming up, the website is just black).

MARIATORGET

Leaving Hornstull, you can either take the scenic route towards Skanstull, walking along the water past the park Tantolunden where you'll find even more garden allotments and boats along the way, or you can crisscross your way east towards Mariatorget. Choosing the latter, make sure you stumble upon Krukmakargatan. Anything but picturesque, it offers a great deal of other pleasures.

Browse through Stockholm's best selection of luxurious magazines, inspiring films and art books at **PAPERCUT** (Krukmakargatan 24-26), you'll leave feeling a tad more interesting than you did when you entered.

Once having refreshed the mind, do the same for your wardrobe in one of the fashionable shops next door, **NITTY GRITTY** being a long-term (albeit expensive) favourite.

A bit further down the street, pop into **HERR JUDIT** (Brandstationen, Krukmakargatan 22), a disused fire station abundant with quirky and beautiful vintage treasures. Try on some extravagant jewellery or imagine what the hippo sculpture might do for your living room.

Should the urge for a coffee break become pressing, you are in the right area. Only 40 metres from each other, two of Sweden's best coffee places battle it out on a daily basis: **DROP COFFEE** (Wollmar Yxkullsgatan 10) and **JOHAN & NYSTRÖM** (Swedenborgsgatan 7). Both make great coffee. Both offer seats in the sun.

But while Johan & Nyström has more of a connoisseur approach to their coffee (without being snobbish about it), Drop Coffee is a little more relaxed. They also put up a great breakfast featuring their trademark fruit and nut bread (that will convince even the most avid fruit-does-not-belong-in-bread believer).

Mariatorget. Really the heart of this part of Söder, Mariatorget is a cute little park/square where you'll find a cross-section of all the people living on the island. Worth a stroll, but avoid the open-air cafés lining its sunny side; they are both underwhelming and overpriced.

If you are into details when it comes to interior decorating, check out the alternative hardware store **BYGGFABRIKEN** (Högbergsgatan 29). Really passionate about building conservationism, they manufacture and stock genuine light fixtures, cords, doorbells, hasps, tiles, hooks and so on, exactly as they looked from the turn of the last century through to functionalism. The feeling of having stepped right into an old country store is an extra bonus of course.

SOFO (SOUTH OF FOLKUNGAGATAN)

As Folkungagatan should generally be avoided, instead choose the inconspicuous Kocksgatan. Narrow and a bit dodgy, it has never drawn much of a crowd – that is until recently when small shops started to pop up one after the other. Among them is **ESKI KILIM** (Kocksgatan 25), a kilim rug gallery. The welcoming and enthusiastic owner will gladly tell you interesting stories about the different rugs and might even offer you a glass of wine.

If you're in the mood for cooking up something delicious, you won't be short of choices. Peruse the shelves of oriental-inspired Aubergine (Nytorgsgatan 25) or head straight for Stockholm's holy grail of food inspiration: **CAJSA WARG** (Renstiernas gata 20). However, you don't really need a kitchen to enjoy a visit here – pick up some cheese and cold cuts and head to Vitabergsparken. Take the wooden stairs up and continue towards Sofia kyrka until you have a splendid view over the south of Stockholm, and voilà!

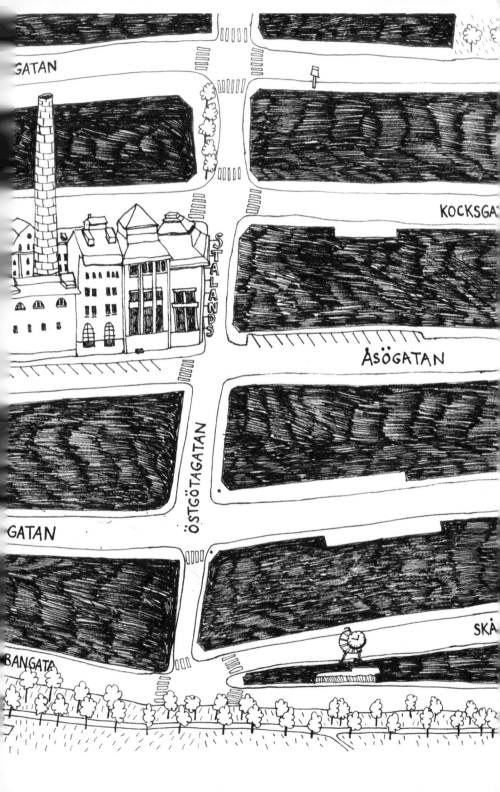

You really can't write a piece about SOFO without mentioning Nytorget – its epicentre. On a warm day, the small park and its surrounding cafés, restaurants and bars get filled to the brim with twenty-to-thirty-going-on-forty-somethings working (or posing) as designers, musicians and writers. Although it's easy to rant about the somewhat anxious pursuit of cool that is omnipresent in SOFO in general, really, this is a great area completely littered with shops, cafés (try **IL CAFFÈ**, Södermannagatan 23) bars and restaurants.

For the cosiest Nytorget experience, elbow your way into the tiny and quaint tapas place **SARDIN** (Skånegatan 79) where the helpful owner will more often than not magically find you a seat. Be sure not to leave until you've had the scrumptious bacon-wrapped dates (but mind the stone inside). They don't take reservations so be there early to increase your chance of getting a table.

For an evening walk, leave all others behind and head down Katarina Bangata, past Ringvägen (which marks the southern border of SOFO) until you get to the slightly hidden street Blecktornsstigen on your right hand side. A residential street, it wiggles its way up past lush bushes and trees until you get to the beautiful red and yellow houses, playing hide and seek from the world. Walk through the lovely inner courtyards and feel like you are in a small town in the 1930s. As you approach the end of the street, an old manor house, Stora Blecktornet, will appear. Quietly discover its pretty garden, smelling of summer and countryside, and if you are lucky, you may suddenly find yourself standing face to face with a roe deer.

FASHION STORIES

TEXT: **LOTTA LEWENHAUPT**
PHOTOGRAPHY: **VIKTOR GÅRDSÄTER**

It is a well known fact that Swedes are very trend-conscious, something which can easily be seen in the city centre of Stockholm.

One of the liveliest areas in the city is around the pedestrian shopping street of Biblioteksgatan, where you not only find some of the most popular restaurants and bars in town, but also the best fashion shops in the northern hemisphere. Alongside international labels such as Burberry, Ralph Lauren, Hugo Boss, Gucci, Louis Vuitton and Marc Jacobs you will find Sweden's best known fashion brands, with simple, clean-cut styles by our brightest designer stars. You will quickly discover that 'clean-cut' is as common in Swedish clothes as it is in interior design. I recommend that you take a closer look at some specific labels and really indulge in the oft-seductive atmosphere of the fresh and minimalist shop interiors.

Before I give the addresses to the fashion stores I have picked out, I would like to make a swift introduction to the brands I specialise in.

Swedish fashion designers are really good at no-nonsense, practical, easy-going and affordable design. Fashionable and sexy come as a bonus. But wearability and a sense of timelessness is always more important than being over-the-top. Swedish design could be described as 'classic with a twist'; this is certainly true of brands such as Filippa K, Whyred, Hope and Acne. These brands are constantly updating their collections so new styles match and blend well with older garments. Another important issue is jeans: the best-fitting ones you will find at Acne, Hope, Filippa K and Blk Dnm. I dare say jeans are a Swedish speciality!

When talking about Swedish fashion one can never ignore H&M, the low-budget chain of stores and one of the biggest players on the global fashion scene. Just like competitors Zara or Top Shop, they supply cheap copies of current fashion styles, but H&M really took the idea of 'more fashion for less money' a further step in 2004 when they started collaborating with international designers on a yearly basis; all of a sudden ordinary women could afford brand names like Stella McCartney and Viktor & Rolf.

STAFF AT WHYRED

STAFF AT HOPE

STAFF AT BLK DNM

STAFF AT FILIPPA K

Another step in this direction is to upgrade their own labels: CoS (Collection of Style) could easily be described as low key basics competing with upmarket brands like Ralph Lauren or Hugo Boss; & Other Stories is spot-on, competing with several super trendy upmarket brand labels, with regards to accessories, clothes and makeup. It's all about price worthy fast food fashions. You could say the Swedes cater to all taste buds!

& OTHER STORIES
BIBLIOTEKSGATAN 11
WWW.STORIES.COM

ACNE
NORRMALMSTORG
WWW.ACNESTUDIOS.COM

BLK DNM
MÄSTER SAMUELSGATAN 1
WWW.BLKDNMCLOSEUP.COM

COS
BIBLIOTEKSGATAN 3
WWW.COSSTORES.COM

FILIPPA K
BIBLIOTEKSGATAN 2
WWW.FILIPPA-K.COM

HOPE
SMÅLANDSGATAN 14
WWW.HOPE-STHLM.COM

WHYRED
MÄSTER SAMUELSGATAN 3
WWW.WHYRED.SE

SILENT CIRCULAR

A VISIT TO STADSBIBLIOTEKET

TEXT: **JOSEFIN PALMGREN**

PHOTOGRAPHY: **TOVE FREIIJ**

I've always had a special relationship with books. Even before I could read I was crazy about chewing on them. Pretty much as soon as I passed the chewing phase, I discovered the city library of Stockholm, Stadsbiblioteket. The transition from the rowdy school library and all-the-same-looking football and pony books to the majestic, silent, circular hall at Stadsbiblioteket was bewildering. I felt like I was entering a sacred temple, straight out of one of the fantasy books I was reading at the time. I still get the same feeling every time I walk through the narrow, revolving doors.

The building, an outstanding example of Nordic Classicism, was inspired by the 18th century building Barrière Saint-Martin in Paris. The interior consisted of a grand rotunda rising up several levels, high enough to give the chills to anyone with the slightest acrophobia.

The library holds about 700,000 books, impressive in their diversity and meticulous order. Here you can also run into all kinds of folk, from cookbook enthusiasts, Goethe-inspired teens and the scholarly elderly. You can sneak into the rooms of absolute quiet and peep at the students as they write intensely. You can walk through the kid's section, wishing so hard you'd grown up in this neighbourhood; you'll just have to sit down and dream away in one of the comfy chairs around.

This library is a magical place, worth visiting just to savour the scent of printed ink, old parchment and knitted sweatshirts. Sentiment aside, here are some cool utilities available at the library. Let me list them for you:

1. You can borrow books and read on site. To take them home you need a Swedish address. I strongly advise you to set up an account. All you need to do is to report to the info desk and they will provide you with a library card with which you can borrow books, music, movies and digital books. You can return a borrowed object at any of the regular libraries in Stockholm.

2. You can use the Internet for 30 minutes. You can also hook up your phone or computer to free WIFI.

3. You can hang out at the premises for a bit of calm and fika. The café is not particularly special but it is located inside the most interesting building in Stockholm. My slight dislike for this place is also probably best explained by the fact that the café wasn't there when I was a child.

4. Next to the main library is the Stadsbiblioteket annexet, here you can find a wide collection of old and new magazines, and newspapers in 70 different languages. There are about 3,600 different magazines available here, and you can also gain access to article search.

5. If you're travelling with children, story time in the special story room is a must. The narration is mostly in Swedish, but the cosiness of the room will make up for any language barrier. If comprehension is a must you should pay this place a visit on Sunday at noon, when Swedish children wanting to learn English gather round for songs and rhymes in English.

6. The library offers 15 minutes free juridical advising if you happen to be in any kind of trouble with the law.

7. If you're looking for your roots, this is the place to be. The library offers access to both Genline and SVAR, which will tell you everything about your distant Swedish ancestors.

8. Up and coming entrepreneurs are welcome to participate in seminars about how to lead a company. Perfect for Stockholmare with big dreams.

9. It is possible to book your own librarian and discuss all the bigger literary questions buzzing around in your head, without any time limit.

10. Last but not least you can book a guided tour of the library. This will teach you more about the services of the library and guide you through the art and architecture of Gunnar Asplund, the architect behind Stadsbiblioteket.

Opening hours are generous but vary, so the best thing to do is to check them online at www.biblioteket.stockholm.se. Don't forget to keep as quiet as possible in all areas, except the kids department and the café, and never forget this is holy ground to some.

STOLEN NOTES FROM LITTLE BLACK BOOKS

INSIDER TIPS ON STOCKHOLM ESSENTIALS

SHOP

GAMLA LAMPOR for Swedish and Danish vintage lamps, chairs and industrial objects. (Sibyllegatan 18)

HEDENGRENS BOKHANDEL go downstairs for many pretty books. (Stureplan 4)

PRESS STOP for Apartamento Magazine and other important journals. (Regeringsgatan 27, Fleminggatan 50, Götgatan 31)

STUTTERHEIM RAINCOATS for fitted rain gear. Can be useful. (Åsögatan 132)

LANKA TE OCH KRYDD IMPORT for hot sauces, spices and tea. (Ringvägen 143)

WIJNJAS GROSSHANDEL (Bergsgatan 24), **GAMLA AMSTERDAM** (Hornsgatan 39A) and **ANDROUETS OSTBUTIK** (Nybrogatan 6, Götgatan 39) for cheese.

FOOD/DRINK

REGGEV HUMMUS for hummus and ginger beer. (Ringvägen 145)

LA NETA for Mexican fast food and free access to coriander. (Barnhusgatan 2, Östgötagatan 12B)

AKKI SUSHI at Medborgarplatsen, easier than going to Tokyo. (Folkungagatan 45)

Lunch at **NOBIS HOTEL** in the bistro or at tables outside. Buy FT Weekend in the square. (Norrmalmstorg 2-4)

DAHPNES (Artillerigatan 56), **DEN GAMLE OCH HAVET** (Tulegatan 27), **URBAN DELI** (Nytorget 4) and **NOSTRANO** (Timmermansgatan 13) for mid-week dinners.

RESTAURANG AG for steaks. (Kronobergsgatan 37)

KAFFE for coffee and Västerbotten-toast. No laptops allowed at the counter. (Sankt Paulsgatan 17)

OAXENS SKAFFERI for cold cuts and take away lunch. Preferable in winter when they have soup. (Mariatorget 2)

ALBERT AND JACK'S SKEPPSBRON for sour dough sandwiches and buns. You can borrow a chair and sit on the quay. (Skeppsbron 24)

HÖTORGET. TOVE FREIIJ

CINEMAS

STUREBIOGRAFEN (Birger Jarlsgatan 41a) and **BIOGRAFEN VICTORIA** (Götgatan 67) for critic's choice movies, **COSMONOVA** (Frescativägen 40) for educational fulldome films.

BUILDINGS

CENTRALBADET (Drottninggatan 88) and **KUNGLIGA DRAMATISKA TEATERN** (Nybroplan) for facade admiration.

MUSEUMS

THIELSKA GALLERIET (Sjötullsbacken 8) for Munch and Zorn, **HALLWYLSKA MUSEET** (Hamngatan 4) for the feeling of being totally secluded from the city and **CARL ELDHS ATELJÉ** (Lögebodavägen 10), the home of an artist.

DRY CLEANER

ROYAL KEMTVÄTT & SKRÄDDERI for anything ruined or creased. (Östermalmstorg 4)

PICK UP
(PERISHABLE)

Swedish produced **HONEY**, **KNÄCKEBRÖD** (hard bread), jams like **LINGONSYLT** and **HJORTRONSYLT**, **ELDERFLOWER** squash, **KALLES KAVIAR**, **HERRING** in jars.

(PERMANENT)

RODEO magazine, **BYREDO** perfume, **ACNE** jeans, tin bracelets made by the **SAMI** community, second hand ceramics by **GUSTAVSBERG**, **RÖRSTRAND** and **UPSALA-EKEBY**, retro wooden toys by **BRIO**, a **CHEESE CUTTER** for hard cheese, **JAYS** earphones.

NOBIS HOTEL. TOVE FREIIJ

TRY

WATER from the **TAP**, **BRYGGKAFFE**, **RAGGMUNK**, **SMOKED SALMON FINS** (has nothing to do with the practice of eating shark fins), **NEW POTATOES** with **DILL**, **CHANTERELLES** mushrooms, **KARL-JOHAN** mushrooms (which the Italians call 'Porcini'), **LOCAL BEER**, **FILMJÖLK** with muesli for breakfast.

SLEEP

Apartment rental sites like **AIRBNB.COM** offer places to suit all tastes and budgets, **HELLSTENS MALMGÅRD** (Brännkyrkagatan 110) for a humble and historical vibe, **LYDMAR HOTEL** (Södra Blasieholmshamnen 2) for urban gentlemen, **GRAND HOTEL** (Södra Blasieholmshamnen 8) for flash folk and pop stars, **ETT HEM** (Sköldungagatan 2) for your wedding night.

CONTRIBUTORS

REBECKA BEBBEN ANDERSSON IS A SWEDISH ARTIST, SET DESIGNER AND ARCHITECT. SHE WORKS WITH SCULPTURE, PERFORMANCE AND COLLAGE. SHE IS CURRENTLY FOCUSED ON MAPS AS STORIES AND EXAMINING THE POWER OF THE PUBLIC ROOM. MOST OF ALL SHE WANTS TO SWIM ALL SUMMER LONG.

JOHAN BARRETT IS A SWEDISH/AMERICAN ILLUSTRATOR AND GRAPHIC DESIGNER. HE GREW UP WITH ONE FOOT IN EACH COUNTRY, BUT NOW WORKS AND LIVES ON THE ROYAL HUNTING GROUNDS OF NORRA DJURGÅRDEN IN STOCKHOLM.

SANDRA BEIJER IS AN AUTHOR, BLOGGER AND COLUMNIST. SHE HAS LIVED IN LONDON, NEW YORK AND PARIS BUT IS CURRENTLY LOCATED IN HER HOMETOWN STOCKHOLM. SANDRA IS OBSESSED WITH SCRABBLE, HANDSOME, YOUNG MEN, LIGHT BEER AND THE SMELL OF STOCKHOLM DURING EARLY SUMMER.

EDWARD BLOM IS A WELL-KNOWN SWEDISH RADIO AND TV PERSONALITY, WHO FREQUENTLY GIVES LECTURES ON FOOD AND DRINK HISTORY. HE APPEARS IN NUMEROUS TV SHOWS, AS WELL AS ON RESTAURANT AWARD JURIES. HE IS ALSO A FELLOW WRITER AT THE CENTRE FOR BUSINESS HISTORY IN STOCKHOLM WHERE HE WAS EMPLOYED FROM 1997 TO 2012 AS AN ARCHIVIST, EDITOR, AND HEAD OF SPECIAL PROJECTS. IN SEPTEMBER 2013, HIS LIFESTYLE BOOK, ALLTING GOTT OCH ALLDELES FÖR MYCKET (EVERYTHING GOOD - AND PLENTY OF IT), WILL BE PUBLISHED BY NORSTEDTS.

CARL JACOB TOMAS BOHLIN IS A PURPOSEFULLY DIRECTIONLESS DREAMER AND PROUDLY DISPASSIONATE DILETTANTE OF JAZZ IMPROVISATION. SOMEWHAT ELUSIVE, HE IS MOST EASILY SPOTTED AT TWILIGHT, ELEGANTLY EVADING HIS SWORN ENEMY 'MEANINGFULNESS'. MAIL HAS BEEN SENT FOR HIM TO ADDRESSES IN STOCKHOLM SINCE 2004.

KATARINA BOHLIN WENT FROM ÖREBRO WITH LOVE, TO PARIS AND THEN STOCKHOLM. NOW GOING ON HER THIRD YEAR IN STOCKHOLM SHE IS ELBOWS DEEP IN THE SOURDOUGH BUSINESS, STILL UNABLE TO FIND THE CAFÉ OF HER DREAMS OR A TRUSTWORTHY HAIRDRESSER.

MATTIAS BÄCKLIN IS A MULTIMEDIA ARTIST BASED IN STOCKHOLM WHOSE MAIN FOCUS IS DRAWING, GRAPHICS AND VIDEO. WHEN ABSENT FROM HIS STUDIO, HE IS EITHER BIRD WATCHING OR BREAKDANCING.

OSCAR CARLSON IS AN ARTIST AND A WRITER. AT SOME POINT HE MADE HIS WAY BACK TO STOCKHOLM AFTER SEARCHING FOR TRUTH IN LONDON AND FRANKFURT. THE TRUTH HAS BEEN EVASIVE BUT SO IS CARLSON. THEY KEEP A SAFE DISTANCE.

JIMMY CROONA DISCOVERED THE CAMERA AS A TOOL TO TELL STORIES EARLY ON IN HIS LIFE. HE GRADUATED AS A PHOTOJOURNALIST FROM MITTUNIVERSITET AND HAS WORKED AS A FREELANCE DOCUMENTARY PHOTOGRAPHER AND STAFF PHOTOGRAPHER AT VARIOUS SWEDISH NEWSPAPERS.

JOE DALY IS A PART IRISH PART ICELANDIC COLLECTOR OF LANGUAGES. BASED IN LONDON, HE SPENDS SUMMERS IN STOCKHOLM AND WINTERS IN REYKJAVÍK. JOE BEGAN HIS FIRST PIECE OF FICTION OVER FIFTY YEARS AGO. THERE IS STILL NO END IN SIGHT.

KJELL DOKTOROW IS AN ART DIRECTOR AND PRODIGIOUS HANDBALL PLAYER.

GUSTAV ELLIOT WAS BORN AND RAISED IN STOCKHOLM. HE IS A PHOTOGRAPHER/RE-TOUCHER AND AFTER MANY YEARS AS AN EMPLOYEE IN THE SWEDEN/EUROPEAN PHOTO INDUSTRY, ABOUT TO TAKE HIS FIRST STEPS AS A FREELANCER. HE IS LOOKING FORWARD TO THIS NEW STEP IN LIFE. HAVING SUPPORT FROM FRIENDS AND FAMILY MAKES EVERYTHING EASIER.

TOVE ERIKSEN HILLBLOM IS PART SWEDISH AND PART BELGIAN. SHE HAS A BAD HABIT OF COMPETING WITH OTHER CYCLISTS IN THE MORNING RUSH. SHE WORKS AS A COPYWRITER, LOVES FOOD (APART FROM BELL PEPPERS), WISHES SHE COULD TRAVEL MORE AND HAS A NEW FOUND INTEREST IN SCIENCE.

MATTIAS FORSHAGE IS A BIOLOGIST WORKING IN SYSTEMATIC ENTOMOLOGY AND A POET; HE IS THE CO-FOUNDER AND LONG TIME ACTIVIST IN THE SURREALIST GROUP OF STOCKHOLM SINCE THE 80S.

TOVE FREIIJ IS A STUDENT OF ARCHITECTURE AT THE ROYAL INSTITUTE OF TECHNOLOGY IN STOCKHOLM, WHERE SHE JUST COMPLETED HER SECOND YEAR. SHE DRAWS IN HER SPARE TIME, BUT PREFERS HER CAMERA.

MATS GOTHNIER IS A BIOLOGIST AND ENTHUSIASTIC BIRDWATCHER AND FOR OVER 20 YEARS HAS WORKED WITH NATURE CONSERVATION IN STOCKHOLM BOTH AS A VOLUNTEER, FOR THE MUNICIPALITY AND FOR THE GOVERNMENT. HE IS CURRENTLY A COORDINATOR FOR AN ACTION PROGRAM OF ENDANGERED SPECIES AT LÄNSSTYRELSEN (THE COUNTY ADMINISTRATIVE BOARD OF STOCKHOLM). HE HAS A SPECIAL INTEREST IN THE INTERACTION BETWEEN HUMANS AND ANIMALS IN THE URBAN CITY JUNGLE.

ALISA GRIFO IS THE OWNER OF KIOSK IN NEW YORK CITY. SHE TRAVELS OFTEN FOR WORK AND PLEASURE. TWELVE YEARS AGO SHE MARRIED A STOCKHOLMER AND SINCE THEN HAS LIVED BETWEEN NEW YORK AND STOCKHOLM.

VIKTOR GÅRDSÄTER IS A STOCKHOLM-BASED PHOTOGRAPHER AND ARTIST. HE HAS JUST RELEASED HIS FIRST CHILDREN'S BOOK AND WHEN HE ISN'T TAKING PICTURES YOU CAN FIND HIM ON A FOOTBALL FIELD OR AT A CONCERT.

ALEXANDER HAVELDA HAS A DEGREE IN POLITICAL SCIENCE, IS A MUSICIAN, TOURIST GUIDE, TRAVEL AGENCY OWNER, PR CONSULTANT AND TENNIS INSTRUCTOR. HE LIVES IN STOCKHOLM AND PRAGUE, LIKES SOUL MUSIC, AND IS ONE OF THE LEADERS OF THE CZECH FOOTBALL TEAM BOHEMIANS 1905'S SWEDISH SUPPORTER GROUP VEPROVY CREW.

KRISTIN LARSSON IS AN ASSISTANT BUYER AT H&M AND LIKES BREAKFAST IN BED.

ANNE LAURELLA WORKS AS BOTH PUBLISHER AND EDITOR. SHE HAS WORKED IN THE PUBLISHING WORLD FOR 17 YEARS AND IS PART OWNER OF LAURELLA & WALLIN, A PUBLISHING HOUSE THAT PUBLISHES BOOKS ABOUT TRAVEL AND HISTORY. SHE LIVES IN KUNGSHOLMEN, BUT CAN BE SPOTTED IN ROME AND IN THE SOUTH OF FRANCE WHEN IN NEED OF SUN, A GOOD GLASS OF WINE OR A STRONG ESPRESSO (AND THAT IS QUITE OFTEN …).

LOTTA LEWENHAUPT IS AN AUTHOR, EDITOR AND LECTURER WHO HAS BEEN WORKING WITH SWEDISH FASHION AND DESIGN MAGAZINES SINCE THE LATE SIXTIES; SHE IS CURRENTLY BLOGGING FOR ELLE INTERIÖR, WHERE SHE WAS ONCE MANAGING EDITOR FROM 1994 UNTIL 2011; SHE LIKES TO CALL HERSELF A 'FASHION-PASSIONISTA' AND SPECIALISES IN 20TH CENTURY FASHION AND DESIGN; SHE HAS PUBLISHED SEVERAL BOOKS, THE LATEST BEING BILDEN

AV MODET (ABOUT SWEDISH FASHION-PHOTOGRAPHY, BOKFÖRLAGET ARENA, 2009) AND SUPPLIED THE TEXTS FOR THE LIFESTYLE BOOK ATT LEVA MED KONST & DESIGN (BLADHBYBLADH, 2012).

BILLIE LINDAHL IS AN ARTIST AND MUSICIAN WITH A DEGREE IN AESTHETICS, WHO SPENDS HER TIME WRITING AND COLLECTING SONGS, TRAVELLING, DEEJAYING AND HANGING AROUND RECORD SHOPS AND CONCERT HALLS. SHE IS CURRENTLY WRITING MUSIC FOR AN ART EXHIBITION AND MAKING ALBUMS WITH HER BANDS PROMISE AND THE MONSTER AND STIU NU STIU.

INKA LINDERGÅRD (B.1985, FINLAND) AND **NICLAS HOLMSTRÖM** (B.1984,SWEDEN) LIVE AND WORK IN STOCKHOLM BUT TRAVEL TOGETHER, SEEKING PLACES TO CONTINUE THEIR PRACTICE OF CREATING DIFFERENT REPRESENTATIONS OF NATURE, USING THE PHOTOGRAPHIC IMAGE TO CAPTURE THEIR LANDSCAPES. THEIR BOOK WATCHING HUMANS WATCHING (KEHRER VERLAG) WON THE SVENSKA FOTOBOKSPRISET IN 2012 AND WAS NOMINATED FOR THE GERMAN DEUTSCHER FOTOBUCHPREIS 2013. THEY ARE REPRESENTED BY SWEDISH PHOTOGRAPHY, BERLIN.

EMELIE LINDGREN GREW UP IN THE FORESTS OF NORTHERN SWEDEN BUT HAS FOUND A HOME IN STOCKHOLM, IN THE AREA LINO (LITTLE NORRLAND) IN SÖDERMALM (NO JOKE). WHEN SHE IS NOT WORKING AS PRODUCTION MANAGER AT A PHOTO AND RETOUCH STUDIO SHE CHALLENGES HERSELF WITH YOGA AND STATEMENTS OF WHAT A GOOD SURFER SHE IS GOING TO BECOME. SHE ALSO HANGS OUT WITH HER CURLY FRIENDS AND TRAVELS EXTENSIVELY BUT NEVER WITHOUT GOING BACK TO LINO WITH A SMILE.

MAGDA MARNELL IS AN ILLUSTRATOR, ART HISTORIAN, FASHION DESIGNER AND FAKE SAMI DESCENDANT. SHE LOVES TO SURROUND HERSELF WITH BEAUTIFUL THINGS AND UGLY ANIMALS.

JOHAN NILSSON IS A PHOTOGRAPHER BASED IN STOCKHOLM.

JOSEFIN PALMGREN IS A SWEDISH AUTHOR BORN AND RAISED IN STOCKHOLM. SHE WRITES ABOUT ANGST AND SEX, AND HER GREATEST ENJOYMENT IN LIFE IS BEING WITTY.

SUSANNA PRIETO ÖSTERBERG WORKS AS A LIBRARIAN BY DAY AND SINGS LIKE A LARK BY NIGHT.

PAUL QUANT IS A SWEDISH PROFESSIONAL PHOTOGRAPHER LOCATED IN STOCKHOLM. SINCE 1990 HE HAS WORKED MAINLY WITH ADVERTISING AGENCIES, MAGAZINES AND BOOK PUBLISHERS. SHOOTING PORTRAITS IS ONE OF HIS FAVORITE GENRES.

DEA SARACEVIC IS A DIRECTOR, PHOTOGRAPHER AND TECHNO MUSIC JUNKIE. SHE IS PART OF THE FILM PRODUCTION CREW CALLED MEXICO86. THEY PRODUCE MUSIC VIDEOS, SHORTS, COMMERCIALS AND FUN PROJECTS.

LUDWIG SCHMITZ IS A LITTLE KNOWN MOUNTAINEER WHO AT THE AGE OF 21 MADE AN UNSUCCESSFUL ATTEMPT TO REACH THE SUMMIT OF DER EIGER IN SWITZERLAND. SOON AFTER THE FAILED EXPEDITION, ON WHICH HE HAS SINCE REFUSED TO COMMENT, HE DECIDED ON A NEW PATH AND HOLDS A DEGREE IN COMPARATIVE LITERATURE. TODAY HE IS A LITTLE KNOWN CRITIC FOR PUBLICATIONS LIKE THE DAILY NEWSPAPER DAGENS NYHETER.

SIMON SKUTELI HAS A YELLOW BELT IN JUDO, BUT THIS IS UNKNOWN TO MOST PEOPLE. ONCE UNDER ATTACK, SIMON USED HIS JUDO SKILLS TO THROW HIS OPPONENT FROM ONE SIDE OF HIMSELF TO THE OTHER. THE ANTAGONIST WAS SURPRISED AND COULD NOT BREATHE AS HIS BACK WAS HURT. ALTHOUGH THIS ACCIDENT HAPPENED IN UPPSALA AND NOT IN STOCKHOLM, SIMON BELIEVES THAT STOCKHOLM IS AN EVEN MORE DANGEROUS CITY.

MATHEA SOLHEIM WAS BORN IN 1988 AND GREW UP IN STOCKHOLM. SHE STUDIED LITERATURE AT ASHBOURNE COLLEGE IN LONDON AND AT THE LUND UNIVERSITY, WORKED FOR UNITED NATIONS IN PARIS AND IS NOW STUDYING ECONOMICS AT THE UNIVERSITY OF STOCKHOLM. SHE RESIDES IN ÖSTERMALM IN STOCKHOLM AND WHAT SHE REALLY LOVES IS LITERATURE, FILM AND MUSIC.

KARIN STRÖM IS A NOVELIST, SINGER/SONGWRITER AND JOURNALIST. AFTER SEVERAL YEARS IN LONDON, LOS ANGELES AND NEW YORK SHE NOW RESIDES IN STOCKHOLM. HER DEBUT AT THE AGE OF 20 YEARS OLD WITH THE TRAVELOGUE BENSIN (GASOLINE); RECENT MUSICAL ENDEAVOURS INCLUDE THE BICOASTAL EP NY/LA. KARIN IS ALSO CO-FOUNDER OF THE MINIATURE PUBLISHING COMPANY AGLAKTUQ, WHICH MEANS 'WRITES' IN THE INUIT LANGUAGE INUPIATUN, SPOKEN IN NORTHERN ALASKA.

JENNY SÖDERBERG IS AN ARCHITECT. SHE CURRENTLY TEACHES AT THE SCHOOL OF ARCHITECTURE AT KTH (THE ROYAL INSTITUTE OF TECHNOLOGY). SHE HAS A GREAT INTEREST IN CITIES AND THEIR STRUCTURE, AND LOVES THE EXPERIENCE OF A NEW CITY THROUGH THE WINDOW OF A TAXI BY NIGHT. SHE GREW UP IN MIDTOWN STOCKHOLM, AND KNOWS ITS PULSE AS WELL AS HER OWN.

MÄRTA THISNER IS A PHOTOGRAPHER, WORKING MOSTLY ON PORTRAITS FOR BOOKS AND MAGAZINES. BORN OUTSIDE UPPSALA SHE HAS BEEN A STOCKHOLMER SINCE 2000.

TOMAS TJAJKOVSKI HOLDS AN MBA FROM THE STOCKHOLM SCHOOL OF ECONOMICS AND IS AN ENTREPRENEUR WITH EXPERIENCE IN BRANDING, DESIGN AND ARCHITECTURE. HE IS THE FOUNDER OF SOMMARNÖJEN WHICH DESIGNS, PROJECTS, BUILDS AND FURNISHES HOLIDAY COTTAGES ALL OVER SCANDINAVIA, BRINGING HIM INTO CONTACT WITH MANY OWNERS OF HOLIDAY HOMES IN THE STOCKHOLM ARCHIPELAGO.

THERESE VANDLING WAS BORN IN GOTHENBURG, SWEDEN IN 1980. SHE HAS LIVED IN LONDON SINCE 2000 AND HAS STUDIED AT LONDON COLLEGE OF COMMUNICATION AND AT THE ROYAL COLLEGE OF ART. A GRAPHIC DESIGNER AND ILLUSTRATOR BY TRADE SHE NOW SPENDS MOST OF HER TIME IN HER HACKNEY STUDIO DESIGNING BOOKS AND BOOK COVERS. THERESE IS ALSO A MEMBER OF HERETIC PRINTMAKERS, AN EXPERIMENTAL ILLUSTRATION AND SCREEN-PRINTING STUDIO THAT WORKS ON A WIDE RANGE OF PROJECTS; FROM ART-PRINTS AND GIG-POSTERS, TO RECORD COVERS AND 3-D SOUND INSTALLATIONS.

ISRAEL YOUNG WAS BORN IN 1928 AND IS A NOTED FIGURE IN THE WORLD OF FOLK MUSIC, BOTH IN AMERICA AND SWEDEN. HE IS THE FORMER OWNER OF THE FOLKLORE CENTER IN GREENWICH VILLAGE, NEW YORK, AND SINCE 1973 HAS OWNED AND OPERATED THE FOLKLORE CENTRUM STORE IN STOCKHOLM.

BRITA ÅSBRINK WAS BORN IN STOCKHOLM, HER CURRENT HOME CITY. SHE SEES IT AS A BEAUTIFUL CITY UNDERGOING COMPLICATED CHANGES. SHE HAS WRITTEN A BOOK ABOUT THE NOBEL BROTHERS OIL COMPANY THAT TOOK ROOT IN BAKU, AND THIS IS STILL AN ONGOING INTEREST OF HERS. SINCE THEN SHE HAS WRITTEN SEVERAL BOOKS, ONE ABOUT STOCKHOLM OUTDOOR ART AND ONE ABOUT THE PARK PLANNER HOLGER BLOM.

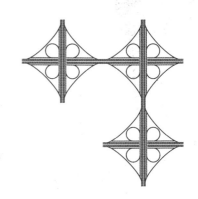
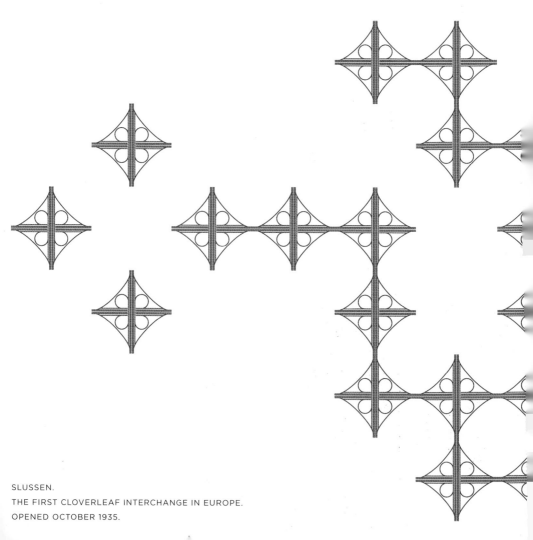

SLUSSEN.
THE FIRST CLOVERLEAF INTERCHANGE IN EUROPE.
OPENED OCTOBER 1935.